New Horizons Edition

The
UNIVERSAL
TRAVELER

a Soft-Systems Guide to Creativity, Problem-Solving, & the Process of Reaching Goals

by Don Koberg & Jim Bagnall

Distribution to the U.S. Trade:

National Book Network, Inc.
4720 Boston Way
Lanham, MD 20706
1-800-462-6420

www.crisp-pub.com

99 00 01   10 9 8 7 6 5 4 3 2

CRISP PUBLICATIONS
1200 Hamilton Court
Menlo Park, California 94025

Library of Congress Cataloging-in-Publication Data

Koberg, Don, 1930-
    The universal traveler : a soft-systems guide to
creativity, problem-solving & process of reaching goals / by
Don Koberg & Jim Bagnall. — New horizons ed.
        p.   cm.
    Rev. ed. of: The all new universal traveler, Rev.©1981.
    Includes bibliographical references and index.
    1. Problem solving.   2. Creative ability.   3. Goal
(Psychology) I. Bagnall, Jim. II. Koberg, Don, 1930-
All new universal traveler. III. Title.
BF441.K55 1991   158'.1—dc20   91-18321
    ISBN 1-56052-045-0   CIP

DIRECTORY

How The UNIVERSAL TRAVELER Can Help You !

The **UNIVERSAL TRAVELER** is designed to serve as a general guide to behaving creatively in a fast-changing world. We believe that it is generally applicable to all sorts of problem situations in any area of endeavor because of its non-specific approach. It can help you deal with life's various events more effectively and creatively as well as alter your status from **tourist** to that of an **explorer**- someone capable of setting new goals and cutting fresh paths to old destinations.

Like other travel guides, **'The Traveler'** can help you plan your many (problem-solving) voyages to both familiar and strange places. Its itinerary for solving or resolving any type of goal or problem systematically includes varied options for making your journeys more enjoyable and meaningful. Plus, it can help make those trips more creatively satisfying. In the end, it remains your job to understand how systematic thinking can work for you, to fill-in the specifics and select the best way(s) to get where you want to go.

This book has three parts:

PART ONE: CREATIVE TRAVEL and FITNESS CENTER is where you can 'tool-up' to embark on ever-more satisfying problem-solving excursions. It includes introductory and general background information regarding the "whats" and "whys" of pro-active thinking, problem-solving, process, creativity, and personal involvement along with a plan for how you can learn to "make your dreams come true."

PART TWO: MISSION CONTROL serves as the 'briefing and trip-planning' center. It contains a universally adaptable strategy for reaching goals, realizing intentions and dealing with adverse situations; including a step-by-step, easy-to-follow guide for managing specific personal problem-solving adventures, along with many general "how-tos" of creative problem-solving. **Mission Control** is where you'll become oriented to your overall trip plan and make preparations for take-off.

PART THREE: SIDE TRIPS, includes games, ideas, suggestions and general information designed to stimulate your enjoyment and to encourage your developing creative behavior. Here, you'll find many additional ways to simplify your creative problem-solving education and help you design a more satisfying life composed of ever more self-controlled and memorable events.

Note: Please write in this book:

If you bought it, it's yours. Why not get the most from it? It has been designed with ample blank space to provoke you to experiment. Reading and listening attentively are important to learning, of course. But remember that both of those learning methods are indirect in the sense that their content comes from someone else...not from you!

True learning and growth doesn't occur until readers or listeners begin to test the validity of what they've read or heard. Only by adding personal comments which either paraphrase or question the information received, can you become personally involved. And each time you 'participate' in some way, the value of your work increases for you. So, please add notes, sketches, and examples of your own to this book. Alter the illustrations or paste-in new ones. Don't just scratch out what you disagree with. Change it to reflect your own views.

BON VOYAGE!
(Don't forget to write!)

PART ONE
CREATIVE TRAVEL
and
EXPEDITION
FITNESS
CENTER

Preparing for your
Creative Problem-Solving Voyages

THE KNACK FOR CREATIVE TRAVEL

**CREATIVITY ASPECTS OF PHYSICAL
AND MENTAL HEALTH**

BECOMING A SELF-MANAGING NAVIGATOR

DISCOVERING PROCESS

**MAP-READING: TRAVELING THE PROCESS PATH
TO SUCCESS**

GENERAL TRAVEL AND LANGUAGE GUIDES

INTRODUCTION

A **major difference** between novices and experienced travelers is that old-timers expect the unexpected and ready themselves to meet it; whereas, newcomers are rarely prepared as they rush impulsively ahead into unfamiliar territory.

Seasoned Travelers are **planners**. They buy guidebooks, read about the people and places they intend to visit, make reservations, and generally lineup the key elements for a successful trip. Before departure they pack carefully, making sure to take along everything they'll need and little more. Without lots of unnecessary goods to worry about and slow them down, they travel far more efficiently and enjoyably than those starting out for the first time.

Beginners, on the other hand, aren't so creative. They tend to learn the hard way; often **wishing** they'd been smarter before leaving on a costly voyage overburdened with lots of useless baggage. It's usually not until afterwards that they begin to discover what they could have done up-front to reduce the high cost of their travels later on. Although vowing that "next time" they'll be ready for any mishap instead of 'blasting-off' unprepared, they rarely record their plans for improvement...and end up having to relearn the same lessons over and over again.

Here, in the **CREATIVE TRAVEL and EXPEDITION FITNESS CENTER**, you'll find the basic requirements for embarking on any type of creative problem-solving journey. In one light-weight package, it contains all you'll need for the entire process of successfully and enjoyably getting ready, getting there, and getting back.

CREATIVE PROBLEM-SOLVING AND GOAL-ATTAINMENT

The Life Process as a Creative Journey

The 'process of life' is generally measured in stages or events. As we become more aware of being in charge of that step-by-step process, we begin to improve our movement between its stages. As self-navigators, we set our courses and overcome barriers as we strive to reach them.

Learning to live life more creatively, i.e., constructively different from normal, is no secret. Every normal person already knows how to behave in unusual ways. The difficult part comes with knowing when to behave that way, developing the freedom to actually do it, and gaining expertise (knowledge, attitude, and skill).

Problem-Solving is part of living. The general definition of 'a **problem**' is '**a condition or situation in need of change or repair**'. We are all part of the same changing and developing imperfect existance. In dealing with life, everyone is forced to be a problem-solver. Some people just do it better; i.e., more constructively and/or more enjoyably than others. That's where creative behavior or design comes into the picture.

Creativity is identified by behavior. Behaving creatively is not only a key part of being professional; it's also a measure of how highly one's professional services are eventually valued. To professional problem-solvers, the act of **design** implies creativity. It describes the **activity** or **process** of creative problem-solving. Another word for **process** is **sequence**; i.e., a series of interrelated actions or events. Professionals are conscious of process and behavior.

The literature on the subjects of design process and creativity contains literally dozens of documented methods and procedures outlining the creative solving of problems. **Creative problem-solving** is synonymous with **design process**; *a sequence of unique actions leading to the realization of some aim or intention.*

Developing a Knack for Behaving Creatively

The word **'creativity'** implies a difference; an inventiveness; a **uniqueness**. Creativity is a term we all use to define unusual behavior; those **unique**, but still acceptable activities which differ from what is normal or expected. In a nutshell **creative behaviors** are unique, atypical, and beyond normal.

The term 'unique' is generally used to express something more than mere newness. We expect the unique to be 'truly new' i.e., to go beyond our current understanding; to in some way be an eye-opener, a step forward; to include some kind of constructive, progressive content. What we actually mean when we use the term **creativity** is '**behavior** which is **constructively different** from what we would normally expect'. In short, Creativity is probably best described as **constructive extraordinary behavior**.

Learning to behave creatively requires awareness and effort to control behavior instead of being a mere bystander in the life process. Like many possible "good intentions", accepting the challenge of behaving differently from others is often easier to say than do.

As we observe creative problem-solvers in action, they seem to glide through the situations which confront them. They appear to bound easily over all barriers and seem able to handle any issue easily. They appear always quick to do and say things which get to the heart of any problem faster than others. They seem to be **clear thinkers**. We pay attention to the unusual results they produce. We admire and often envy their ability and we tend to think of them as being **special** people...as having a certain **'knack'** that others lack.

Although their creative behaviors aren't always noticably different from normal behaviors, these special people always seem to be doing the **'wrong' things** and getting the **'right' results**. Not only do they "get away with murder", they also seem to get what they want from life. We'd like to imagine them as being lucky or 'gifted'; as being somehow 'blessed' in ways that the rest of us missed out on somewhere along the line. But, the truth, of course, is that, **creative people** are **no luckier** (or more blessed) than others...with few exceptions. They have merely learned to **make their own 'luck.'** Their **abnormal** behavior works **for** them instead of **against** them. They can quickly identify what they want and do what it takes to go after it. They are merely **normal people who behave abnormally when necessary.**

By contrast, **other** people seem to always need a boost. They struggle to achieve even the smallest aims. For them, getting closer to what they might want is a constant battle. Even their wants are vague. Without clear goals or knowledge of how to reach them, they're always at a loss for what to do next. The result? They replace work with worry, spend much of their energy getting nowhere, and are not very satisfied with their life. Sound familiar?

The difference is surely not determined by birthrights. Becoming more of a **self-starter** isn't reserved for only a special few. Anyone can learn to be more creative. It's all in **knowing a few basic behaviors and developing a constructive, active** point of view. Analysis of any of the dozens of so-called "success courses" being offered today, shows the focus to be on two ever-essential issues: **knowledge** (knowing what it takes) and **attitude** (self-belief, plus a willingness to get started).

For most people, the desire to include more creativity in what they do is like dreaming of an excursion to a mysterious, uncharted, far-off destination. Few people ever realize such fantasy. But, dreams can be made to come true. **Getting to any intended destination is just a hop, skip, and jump from where you are right now.** The path has been clearly marked by many previous travelers who have returned from their adventures into once uncharted regions of creative problem-solving to share vivid descriptions of what you might expect along the way.

HOP

ground track

Runway

SKIP

JUMP

HOP-SKIP-JUMP FLIGHT PATH

MENTAL and PHYSICAL HEALTH
Developing and Maintaining Healthy Minds & Bodies for Creative Problem-Solving

Physical and mental health can be important factors when trying to deal creatively with the many strange, often complex problems we face in our lives.

Have you ever heard people say things like "I couldn't enjoy Paris because I had a cold the entire time" or "I wish I could pull myself out of bed to get started on this goal of mine?" Of course you have. But, colds can usually be prevented or managed. And a will to win is certainly acquired by self-control. Clearly, physical and mental fitness for the task at hand is critical to success.

If the adage **"an ounce of prevention is worth a pound of cure"** is valid, then preparing for travel by getting both physically and mentally 'fit' makes sense. NASA's Astronaut Training Program is a definitive example of people preparing for fool-proof travels. No one questions the importance of fitness on journeys into space where allowance for error is obviously very small. But, to the average person embarking on everyday ventures, preparation doesn't seem so essential... until it's too late.

Gain Strength - Avoid the Pitfalls

Healthy minds and bodies are generally developed and maintained by a collective method known and practiced as **preventative maintenance**.

Those who are fit and well-prepared for life's process tend to actively maintain their creative problem-solving strengths. Because of their interest in fitness, they are typically better able to resolve problematic situations with greater success. We call it **"having a positive attitude."**

Strength is normally an advantage; a 'plus' factor. It implies **power**. When appropriately used, being strong tends to simplify any task. Everyone would like to be stronger but, conscious, intentional, building up of strength isn't normal. Weakness is far more commonly expressed in our behaviors. Working toward building up creative problem-solving strength is still somewhat of a unique (creative) behavior: it's one of those 'constructive abnormalities.'

A more typical approach is to bypass preparation in the rush to get the problem solved ('out of the way'), and return to status quo as quickly as possible. We tend to say "There's **no time** to get ready, or get set—we've just got to **go**." And, of course, when the focus is on speed instead of quality, enjoyment or personal education, fitness for the task is easily side-tracked.

You don't have to be nuts to behave creatively... As a matter of fact, it doesn't even help.

Another cause for a general lack of readiness is that it's not always clear that the energy spent in fitness-training will actually result in greater profits later on, i.e., preparation tends to seem like work without a guaranteed payoff. Here, the need to develop personal interest and a positive attitude are again key ingredients. We can be coerced or intimidated, but making decisions to gather information, to develop useful skills, to eat a well-balanced diet, to build a variety of problem-solving muscles, etc. are nearly always personal perogatives.

The basic **strengths** needed for creative problem-solving can be summarized in a few terms:

Awareness
Curiosity and appreciation of life and living

Passion
Zealous love of the quest and determination to interact with life and its events

Self-Control
Taking charge of one's own behaviors

Each of these strengths is a valuable asset by itself. But, when combined, the three unite to become an **abnormally powerful force**.

Awareness

Children are forever amazing adults with their apparently unique awareness of the basic details of life. Forgetting that children must be sensitive to life's patterns and details in order to learn and develop, we instead imagine that their behavior is intentional and, therefore, creatively unique. We delight in a child's fearless experiments with what we have grown to accept as fact, and tend to wish we had their freedom. Kids, however, don't think of one another as behaving more or less creatively. To a child, other kids are merely behaving normally, while adults, who were once fearlessly sensitive children themselves, learn to put aside life's 'details' in order to see bigger pictures...thereby missing much of life's delights.

Developing a keen alertness to life and its many facets is a paramount characteristic of creative behavior. It's another of those necessary and constructive behavioral 'abnormalities.' But being aware of life wasn't always so abnormal. It is a natural human behavior which children depend on for intellectual growth and which we normally stop using and improving with adulthood. Adult awareness involves controlling the **bi-modal brain function** of quickly alternating between <u>sensing</u> reality and <u>knowing</u> what is sensed.

There are at least **three levels of awareness**:
The basic level is **recognition** (acknowledgement of a situation or thing); the second level is **sympathy** (caring about the situation or thing); and the third level is **empathy** (deep personal sharing of the attributes of the situation or thing). All three levels are learnable and controllable.

Becoming aware of another person, for example, might start with recognizing a name, obvious physical features and other identifying details; then, into a deeper level of sympathizing with their peculiar aspects and behaviors, such as seeking out important common interests, and finally, into the deepest sensory level of empathy; i.e., actually feeling the joys and pains of the other (sometimes referred to as 'being in love').

Enthusiasm

Wanting something badly enough is often all it takes to make that dream come true. Active devotion to purpose is undeniably special. Yet, the more typical reaction to most of life's situations can best be described as wishful, rather than assertive. Being

No one is without awareness...some people are just more curious than others.

If being unique is what you seek, re-learning childhood awareness skills should definitely become part of your fitness agenda.

15

zealous about getting what we want is clearly a unique attitude; another creative plus-factor.

Enthusiasm for solving a problem situation or for reaching a goal stimulates a **collective sense of purpose**. It brings all of one's energies together for success. It creates inertia of its own that's hard to restrain. Such an **internal spirit** of profound concern is crucial to entering any arena of competition with intentions of winning. It is an essential ingredient of political competition, athletic challenge, and of course, deep-seated religious beliefs. Like keeping a fire alive by adding fuel and regulating the damper, passion also needs regular rejuvenation and management.

The basic fitness program for stirring-up and/or rekindling enthusiasm involves understanding the human need for rewards. People need some sort of gratifying pay-off or incentive for their efforts. And rewards come in a wide variety of forms with an equally broad range of effectiveness. Similar to moving a stubborn donkey, some of us get up and keep going with rewards of mere 'carrots', while others respond only when prodded with a 'stick' (punished). Where a 'pep talk' might work to excite half a team, the other members may need more tangible stuff. Awareness of the various kinds of 'rewards' or 'threats' you need to keep going on your own strange and perilous voyages can save lots of time and energy. It's all a matter of foresight.

Self-Control (Habit Management)

An essential key to becoming fit as a **navigator** is an ever-developing ability to **make and break habits**.

Self-Control is the **ability to manage one's habits**. And habits are merely repeated behaviors. Creative behavior often involves up-grading or replacing old behaviors with new, better behaviors. The trick is to identify those behaviors considered to be creative and then allow ourself the freedom to begin practicing them. The first part is simpler than the second. Knowing that curiosity is essential for gaining insight doesn't make it easy to overcome older, established, question-blocking behaviors.

Habit-making is a proven habit-breaking method. Try focusing on achieving a positive new behavior instead of fretting over dumping an old one.

Creative behavior hinges on being holistic...being all, instead of only half, of what you can be.

Hindsight is usually more expensive than foresight.

Most of our habits are of our own making. We design them to simplify life in some way. When they stop working for us, who is more authorized to improve or replace them than ourselves?

"Passengers on flights that last an hour or longer can suffer from swollen feet, backache, muscle tension or a feeling of excessive fatigue that manifests itself during the flight or later... Exercise can alleviate some of these ills." Airline Fitness Expert

Stopping old behaviors becomes easier when we realize that a focus on new behaviors leaves no time or attention for the old ones. **Habit-breaking is a paradoxical term**; it suggests the "stopping" of a "doing"; a contradiction in terms. Starting a new behavior is far easier. You **can't stop watching** TV, but you **can start reading** a magazine. You **can't stop worrying** about writing a speech, but you **can start writing an outline**. It's a similar situation with trying to stop drinking alcohol, taking drugs, smoking, nail-biting and other 'bad habits' that are all much easier to 'replace' than to "stop."

Passing the 'Physical'

Maintaining physical fitness is no secret. Age, sex, weight, height, genetic composition, and environment are known influences in everyone's uniquely individual total health potential. We know that it's not merely accidental or unfortunate that some people are unhealthier than others. Again, it's a matter of 'preventative maintenance.' Healthy people are simply better prepared for their particular adventures. They have stamina, i.e., 'staying power'. They are able to travel longer, harder, and farther than others who are less physically capable. They are less held back by their own 'anchors' and tend to advance abnormally faster than others.

Eating appropriate types and amounts of foods and supplements, getting sufficient exercise and rest, dressing in harmony with climatic changes, staying within allowable limits of stress: those are the primary physical qualities of **a healthy traveler**. Inattention to any one of such fundamental concerns can result in 'misfortune' or 'accident'. So, by simply remaining aware of their need for regular physical (and mental) maintenance, creative problem-solvers carry fewer 'extra problem' loads on their travels.

There is no single method for achieving a state of well-balanced health. Literally hundreds of books claim to light the way. A common thread does exist, however. You guessed it: positive attitude- a sincere desire to improve the odds for success. The French word *regimen* seems to sum it up: 'an intentional, regular adherance to a plan or set of rules.'

Attitude Adjustment

Negativism is an unnecessary extra load to take along on any trip; it's like tripping on your own feet. It not only slows you down, but also absorbs your energy, misdirects your focus, and causes all sorts of other hassles to make traveling less than satisfying.

Positive Thinking is generally accepted as a basic requisite for success. Starting a problem-solving journey with a **'negative' attitude** isn't very creative. Instinctively, we all know that it's more constructive to begin our adventures with a positive viewpoint.

Yet, guess what? Like so much wishful thinking, having the will to succeed is also uncommon. Most people merely dream of success; **working** for success is still abnormal. The dreams in themselves are positive, but when it's time for a showdown, negative thinking usually replaces the necessary positive actions.

What's worse is that being failure-prone has become commonplace and socially acceptable. In today's society, politeness and humility almost dictate an ongoing apologetic stance for our less-than-perfect knowledge and our undeveloped skills even before attempting to deal with a new or strange problem-solving situation. We 'confess' our faults up-front to supposedly show just how much (or little?) we are aware of our actions and in control of them. "Oh no. Not me, please. I can't sing at all. Well, O.K., I'll try, but don't expect too much."

Behavioral psychologists describe us as having three parts. They say, aside from our physical bodies, **what we are** is a combination of three aspects: **what we know (knowledge)**, **what we believe (attitudes)**, and **what we can do (skills)**. (**Who we are** is still something else. The current view is that, overall, **we are the controllers of our behaviors**; the driving spirits of our total physical and behavioral make-ups.)

What we are is what we know, what we can do, and what we believe. Who we are is something else.

Mental Fitness involves two of our three basic characteristics: **knowledge** and **attitude**, i.e., to be creatively fit, we need both information and a constructive viewpoint. One **or** the other isn't enough. Merely 'wanting' to go is insufficient; we've got to get started and keep moving.

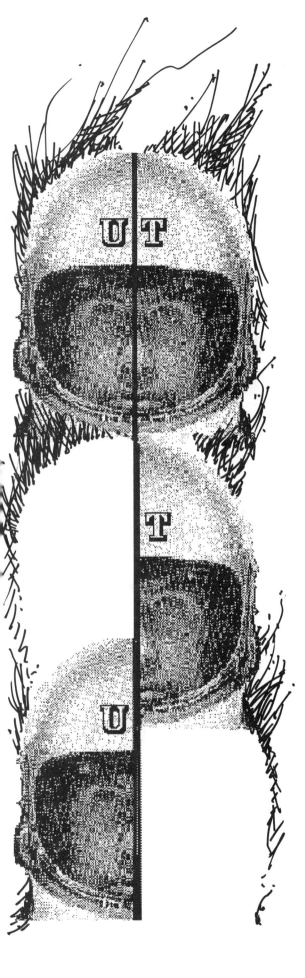

BECOMING A NAVIGATOR:
NOTES ON CREW MANAGEMENT
Mental Organization and Physical Operations

Thinking and **behaving** are natural functions. Everyone thinks and acts. However, "clear thinking" and "creative behavior" are not normal, but special. Logically, we should learn by experience to become aware of our thinking and actions and to direct them toward realizing our intentions and purposes as when trying to solve a problem, attain some goal, reach some objective, or make plans. Unfortunately, learning from experience isn't very efficient. Most people relearn the same things over and over again without ever putting their learning to work for them.

Clear thinkers differ from normal thinkers in that they see both macro- as well as micro-scopically. Their **holistic** approach helps them go beyond the surfaces of things which stop normal thinkers and to comprehend "big pictures" while others see only fragments. This difference in vision leads them to other forms of uniqueness and ultimately to inventiveness.

Research regarding managed self-control suggests what the ancients seemed to know all along: that the **mind controls the brain**. We humans have a **two-part control** relationship consisting of a spirit or **"navigator"** (the mind) and a "crew" of two interrelated, but separately operating, brain functions: a **'thinker'** (normally located within the left hemisphere or so-called "left brain") and a **'sensor/behaver'** (normally located within the right hemisphere and commonly known as "right brain").

In brief, your mentality, the **Navigator**, can control both your thoughts and reasoning as well as your actions and sensitivity.

These two basic human characteristics, although different in many ways, are not mutually exclusive. In fact, working together, they comprise the necessary 'wholeness' of both knowing and feeling which defines overall human activity. When both 'sides of the brain' are healthy and well-developed, they form a dynamic vehicle for a Creative Navigator.

Invention is not a right-brain or left-brain activity; it requires both "sides" of the brain; the whole brain. Also, since **creative behavior** (creativity), by definition, is **a unique or abnormal form of behavior**, it relates to the ultimate human need to progress, to extend the limits of acceptability...to expand or deepen the current understanding and appreciation of life's events and artifacts.

Contrary to popular myths, creative people are neither super heroes nor evil scientists. Nor are they undisciplined weirdos. That's kid stuff. But creative adult behavior **is** intentional, constructive, thoughtful and sensitive to stimulus (aware). It is whole brain, or **holistic**, behavior directed by a keen 'navigator.'

The undisputed **key** to taking personal control of an holistic brain function is **alternation**: the ability to rapidly access both sensing and thinking as needed for dealing with life's ever-changing situations.

Such alternating between sensing and thinking requires understanding the difference between the two brain modes, recognizing which mode is appropriate at any given moment, and developing the ability to activate the appropriate mode when needed. Recognition of our bi-modal human 'control center' has unwittingly led to several popular misconceptions regarding self-control. Commonly used metaphors for describing brain functions often incorrectly portray the Right and Left sides of the brain as **separate and autonomous opponents** rather than as **interrelating complementary components**. Expressions like "sinister left", "feminine right", "uptight left", "playful right", etc., breed other false concepts and ultimately lead to questioning which side is our 'best' side and who or what is actually in charge, when in fact, both are essential.

'Sensitive thinking' continues to come of age with ever-greater knowledge of logic, systematic processes, and use of methodology. Learning to experiment with life is another matter. Remember, as children we once were good at being playful. That skill can be recaptured; it need not atrophy with growing up.

It takes practice to learn to control your own thinking and behavior as a skilled navigator keeps a ship on course...**continual practice**.

If you were to suddenly imagine a truly unique idea, you'd automatically become a minority of one. For a normal person, that's a scary, sobering thought.

FEAR
Arch Foe of Creative Fitness

What stops most people from behaving as creatively as they'd like to?

The answer is **fear**...especially the basic fear of being seen by friends or associates as "silly" or in some way 'less than acceptable.' For a complex set of personal reasons, we each tend to imagine that once we accept the challenge to behave unusually for moments, that we automatically commit our image to the status of "strange." Of course, such poor logic misses the very essence of a creative 'difference.' The weight of fear that some people carry with them is so heavy that they never seem to be able to get started on the journeys they only dream of taking.

When caution turns to fear, the result is negative. It is a true waste of energy; a non-constructive behavior. When normal, feasible cautions become translated into fears, we take on unnecessary loads that can turn the highest of expectations into sad disappointments. On the other hand, where caution is used as a guide for planning, it becomes energy well-spent.

Like other bad habits, it's not really possible to **stop being afraid**. It's only possible to **start** being brave. Whereas fear stems from uncertainty, bravery requires commitment and a strong belief in one's self and one's purposes and intentions. Think about it: Aren't most of the 'creative' people you know full of self-confidence and comparatively fearless in terms of what they allow themselves to do?

The important difference lies in focus. Instead of fearing to be wrong, it's far more positive to try being right. Dreaming of producing unique solutions and reaching satisfying goals is well and good. But, actually making it happen usually stops with the rude awakening that such a 'winner' is also vulnerable to social criticism; a risk that only a few people are willing to take. It remains a fact that, if you want to be seen as "special", you're going to have to behave that way.

Most of our fears are subconscious carry-overs from our childhood when their importance was far greater than it would be today. Their lasting consequence on what we allow ourselves to do in later life tends to go unseen until faced head-on. Learning to reveal, define, and control fear may easily be the most effective way to

It's true that creativity depends on unique, abnormal behavior. But, you don't have to become an "abnormal person" in order to behave abnormally every once in a while.

21

develop and maintain creative fitness. By paying attention to what makes you cautious or threatened or insecure in any way, you'll be better able to plan your creative navigation through most of the hazards in future problem-solving adventures.

Aside from the natural fears of physical threat, injury, or loss of something essential to survival, the most common **fears which hamper creativity are:**

Fear of humiliation: Fear of being laughed at, viewed as a fool or as an incompetent person

Fear of isolation: Fear of being shut out of a peer group or desired social context

Fear of dishonor: Fear of losing the respect of a loved one or friend

BUT, the most common fear of of all is...
Fear of being seen as different from others...paradoxically, a fear of that very same difference which ultimately defines the unique or creative behavior most people long for.

FITNESS IN A NUTSHELL

When preparing for any problem-solving or goal-seeking journey, remember that overall 'creative well-being' combines both physical and mental fitness. The following four-point check-list may help remind you to...

...start becoming an amateur dietition. Learn which foods are good for your particular physical make-up and how food relates to your specific goals and activities

...become a more active, energetic person. If your work keeps you in a chair, get out of it as often as possible. Walk when you can. Don't wait for someone else to do simple physical jobs, like housecleaning. Do 'em yourself. The exercize will provide a bonus atop the other savings.

...size up your dreams and promises and keep them in line with your capabilities and resources. This will not only help you avoid lots of unnecessary stress, but it will also help in developing a self-managing way to greater self-satisfaction.

...think positively; develop a creative viewpoint. Turn life's challenges and problems into adventures. Seek enjoyment from the 'simple pleasures' of curiosity and experimentation by maintaining a positive attitude. Open new doors; look into new corners; question the fixed and stable; experience the 'abnormal'.

AHA!!
DISCOVERING THE PATH OF PROCESS

The Universal Traveler was born nearly 20 years ago; conceived by a need to simplify and combine an increasing number of explanations and formulae for the creative solving of problems. As university design instructors, our problem was to find ways to help students learn to become creative designers and to see that creativity was both generally applicable in all phases of life as well as learnable; to help them see that creativity was not a mystery or a gift which only a select few might have received as a quirk of being specially born.

We looked at the creative problem-solving techniques of industry and the military. We delved into the philosophic writings of Plato and Descartes. We studied market strategy and advertising analysis methods. Each procedure studied was first divided into separate steps or stages, then placed in a comparative position (analog fashion) with other methods to discover if similarities existed and where they occured. We noted how scientists were prone to discuss the subject as 'systematics', how artists explained it in poetic images, how inventors were often the mystical proponents of chance, how business corporations viewed it as a path to profits and how the military were concerned with strategic planning. By examining and comparing dozens of different authorities on the subject, a common or universal sequence of operations eventually evolved.

In our search for common denominators, we found that although each group studied had its own point of view, they all had a similar goal: to be successful in realizing their intentions...just as we all desire in our separate, personal lives. Although each researcher and philosopher explained it differently, **creative problem-solving** boiled down to be essentially the same to them all: **an intentional process of defining success and setting out to achieve it.**

Two behaviors were commonly implied by all as creative neccessities:
the need for CURIOSITY... an ever-developing interest in taking things apart to discover what "makes them tick" and
the need to IMPROVE THINGS... a concern for being constructive; a drive to make things "tick" better.

23

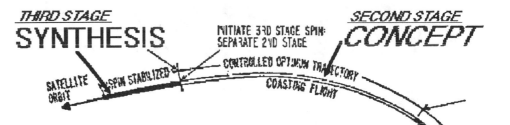

THIRD STAGE
SYNTHESIS

INITIATE 3RD STAGE SPIN:
SEPARATE 2ND STAGE

SECOND STAGE
CONCEPT

SATELLITE ORBIT

SPIN STABILIZED

CONTROLLED OPTIMUM TRAJECTORY

COASTING FLIGHT

FIRST STAGE
ANALYSIS

VERTICAL FLIGHT

ZERO-LIFT TRAJECTORY

LAUNCH

First Analysis; then Synthesis

The general conclusion derived from a collective study of many of the various problem-solving procedures and methods is commonly expressed as "**scientific method**," the view that 'design process' includes but two basic operations: **analysis** and **synthesis**. In simpler terms, process studies show that if we wish to deal with any problem scientifically, we must **first examine** it as a situation to discover what's involved, and then, using the resulting knowledge gained by that analysis, **do something to resolve the situation**.

When all of problem-solving is reducible to such a simple **two-step process**, life instantly becomes a good deal easier. Automatically, problem-solving turns from worry to work; energy can then be **directed** instead of **wasted**. There is no more 'wondering where to begin.' Problem-solving stops being a problem in itself; something a priori to be dealt with before getting on to whatever else is really more important.

Process makes it clear 'where to begin': we start by "analyzing" the situation in order to uncover its facts and details with the intent to identify "what needs fixing." Then, after considering the facts and determining what the true issue(s) is (are), we "synthesize" by eliminating, replacing, or changing parts or relationships according to the 'insight' found in analysis.

Once you understand problem-solving and goal-seeking as a **process** (of applying the results of analysis to what is done in synthesis), what remains is simply the details and enjoyment of your work. By knowing just that much and applying it to what you want to achieve in life, you can avoid the anguish of 'flying by the seat of your pants" or operating "in the dark."

Next comes Concepts

Concepts are points of view: the linkpins or **bridges** between the taking-apart and putting-together stages. To have derived a concept is to have extracted some meaning(s) or purpose(s) from a situation. Conceptualization involves identifying the essential or important factors via

24

Creative people are problem-makers before becoming problem-solvers. They tend to seek out the things in life which need their attention instead of waiting around to be confronted by them.

Analysis which are then addressed or acted on in Synthesis. Concept becomes an **intermediate** or **third step** in a design process. Because it reflects personal insight and specific design intent, it is variously referred to as **measurable** or **design objective(s)**, **specifications**, and simply, as **Definition**.

The need for a "conceptual" connection between Analysis and Synthesis suggests that the task of Analysis goes beyond information gathering into the area of direction-seeking and/or goal identifying. Once you determine to become aware of your destinations, further Analysis stops being open-ended. Effort can then be directed to "relevant issues" instead of spent on the mere gathering of additional general information.

Acceptance of the **basic 3-step design process** (Analysis-Definition-Synthesis) removes the **mysteries** of "where to begin" and "what to do first, second and third." Now it's clear. First, **you learn**. Then, **you become conscious of what you've learned**. And, finally, **you apply what you learned**. Simple! With such a 1-2-3 grasp on problem-solving procedure, you might not even want to wait for problems to come to you, but instead, start 'improving' things before they ever "need fixin'."

Taking Synthesis in Steps
Additional simplification of process is possible by breaking Synthesis, normally viewed as a single giant step, into smaller, more managable and achievable parts.

Three logical sub-stages exist within the overall operation of putting something together in an improved form: **(1) Ideation** (generating optional ways to attain or realize the concept); **(2) Decision** (selecting that specific option which best complies with the concept); and **(3) Implementation** (putting the chosen option to work).

To intelligently complete the process, two human development stages are added: **Acceptance**: conscious willingness; finding incentives for becoming involved, and **finally**, **Evaluation**: determining the degree of value or success; getting something back for effort; extracting education from experience.

25

THE SEVEN UNIVERSAL STAGES OF CREATIVE PROBLEM-SOLVING

ACCEPT SITUATION (Commitment): Agreeing to direct sufficient energies toward resolving a particular problem situation or goal; maintaining the necessary momentum to complete the task

ANALYSIS (Research): Gathering sufficient specific and general information to deal effectively with the situation; organizing the pertinent facts and feelings involved for developing a more complete and detailed view

DEFINE (Destination-Finding): Identifying the key issue or issues; determination of primary cause or essence of the problem situation; translating negative problem conditions into viewpoints and/or objectives

IDEATE (Shopping for Options): Finding many possible alternative plans or ways for achieving the stated objectives or realizing stated intentions

SELECT (Decision-Making): Choosing the way; selecting the 'best bets' from the menu of options generated; comparing alternatives with objectives to find an appropriate fit; determining a plan of action

IMPLEMENT (Taking Action): Putting the plan into operation; translating intentions into physical action or form; realization of the expectation or 'dream'

EVALUATE (Assessment): Review of process (means) as compared with products (ends) to determine worth or value received; making plans for future improvement

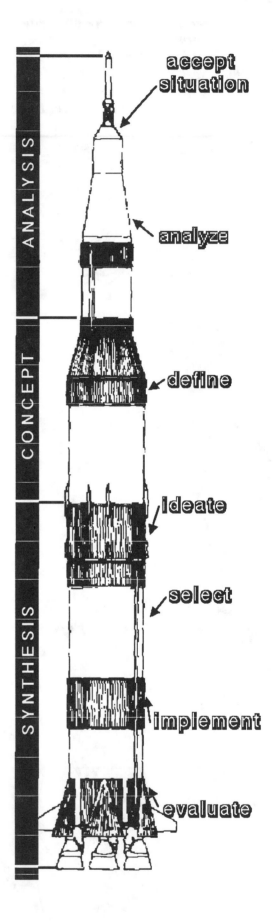

If using the "linear process" seems too basic or restrictive for you, try other patterns.
But, remember that learning to walk by taking one step at a time doesn't mean that you can't eventually learn to hop, skip, jump, and even dance your way to success.

The spectrum of human challenge is broad; nothing is **fixed** about it. Problems and goals come in many forms; each with unique requirements and limitations. This fact often encourages a false impression that a systematic, orderly design process means giving up hopes of ever being truly 'creative' problem-solvers, i.e., the false concept that to be creative, a problem-solver must insist on remaining free from all guides or directions. This, of course, is not too different from wanting to take a trip, but refusing to use a map.

Creative success need not be linear; it is possible in many different ways. Dogged, **linear** step-by-step following of process stages can be limiting in many situations where variation is clearly needed. Using the same seven stages, there are at least **four other ways** to organize their interrelationships. In short, there are freer, more natural, ways to reach destinations. Familiarity with **all five** pathway variations simplifies choosing the one(s) best suited to the varied, separate and unique problem situations in life.

1. **Linear Process:** Step-by-step logical sequence; being cautious of not getting ahead of yourself. Well-suited to large, complex, team projects;

2. **Circular Process:** Starting at any stage and advancing to the others in turn. Ideal for lengthy projects (like college programs, summer jobs, contracts, etc.);

3. **Feedback Approach:** Moving forward while looping back to reconsider previous discoveries. Important when caution is imperative;

4. **Branching Paths**: Allowing specific events and the interrelation of separate stages to control progress ; and

5. **the Natural Pathway:** Awareness of **all stages concurrently**, but emphasis on one or two steps at a time; like viewing seven open boxes in a row, each one ready to receive additional data and thereby modifying your overall thinking accordingly.

The life process itself takes the form of a sprial continuum; an ongoing sequence of events without absolute beginnings or endings; where starting and stopping places are merely imaginary lines of our own making.

Note: If the **linear** approach to design process is similar to a **mule train**, with each unit responsible for pulling the one behind it, then the **natural way** is more like a **horse race** where all units progress independently; where only one unit is 'out in front' (i.e., in focus) at any given moment. The ideal, of course, is to develop a **general process-orientation** to life; one where, enroute to success each stage of living is enjoyed to its fullest , as opposed to the more normal or commonly-held viewpoint of **product-orientation**, where getting to the end is all that's important.

27

MAP-READING:
Following Process
by Using Methods
in Problem-Solving and Goal-Seeking

Though it has been around for many years, **conscious use of process and methodology** in problem-solving or goal-seeking isn't yet commonly practiced. It remains **a reasonably unique, creative behavior**. People behaving normally tend to bypass much of the process in life in favor of "jumping" (directly) from one conclusion to another. In short, it's not normal to undertake a task by making detailed plans and carrying along a set of good tools.

Methods are tools. When there are many different tools available and you know how to use them, problem-solving tasks become simpler and results more satisfying.

Creative problem-solvers, on the other hand, seeing many possibilities and opportunities in life, are more process-aware than product-oriented. They are more likely to stop for at least some analysis before diving into synthesis. They tend to view conscious **procedure** as intelligent map-reading which allows them to tailor a strategy or plan for their problem-solving "operations". Process allows them to see that there are many possible variations in the sequencing of procedural steps as well as many different techniques, or methods for accomplishing each operation step along the way.

Process awareness allows them to see whole areas; including where they're headed and where they've been. It helps to clarify the "big picture" of any goal-seeking or problem-solving adventure; including the location of many possible starting points and destinations as well as all of the landmarks in-between. It makes it easier to determine which routes are best and which to avoid in terms of the special needs or limitations of any situation. Few normal people use maps.

Methodology (the study of mode, means, and technique) allows them to view a spectrum of tools for advancing along their process path. As the old saying goes, "different strokes for different folks." There are as many ways for doing things as there are people to do them. When passing through the analysis step of process, for example, one person might use the 'library' another might 'ask a friend', another might 'make a list.' Still another person might use all three.

Comparing several methods of approach before diving into a task is like searching through a toolbox for suitable hardware before starting a job. But, it takes time.

28

Again, few people have time "to spare." It's far more common to grab for the first tool within reach or to use the same tool for every task 'out of habit' without considering that there might be other or better ways to do things. Some process stages are best acomplished by use of a single method (tool). In other situations, the same stage of process might call for using several methods in concert.

This ever-changing demand makes it important for a creative problem-solver to become familiar with a wide variety of 'ways to do things'. Knowing the names of the various tools in a well-equipped toolbox makes their selection easier. The same is valid with methods. If you can't identify a tool (method) by name, and if you haven't practiced using it, it's going to be difficult to consciously put it to work. Using a claw hammer and nail instead of a tack hammer and brad to hang a lightweight picture, for instance, can easily ruin the surface of the wall.

Since much of what we learn is subconsciously internalized, our education is not too different from the way animals become trained to respond well to things which feel good and to avoid the rest. Thus, most personal techniques remain unconscious and unidentified; difficult to discuss and nearly impossible to call forth or improve. Also, people tend to consider the simple, workable methods they use as personal inventions. To discover that others might use similar techniques is often a let-down. Or worse, to avoid being accused of 'stealing' someone else's secrets, 'personal' methods are usually kept well-guarded and are thereby rarely developed or improved. Consciousness of the menu of methods we use is important so that we might not only improve them, but also be able to add other options to the list when they appear. Larger menus also make it possible for life to become a richer feast!

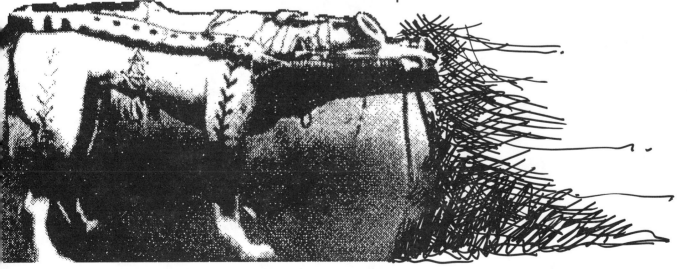

"There's more than one way to skin a cat."

LANGUAGE GUIDE

One of the 'broadening' by-products of travel (and problem-solving) is an increased vocabulary. Learning how other people refer to the same bits of world-wide reality helps in both understanding and decribing those same things in our own language.

Since language is symbolic and merely a translation of reality, it is also separate from reality; a product of imagination. Language seems to work best when it contains many different words for things and the meanings people give to them in order to help us better describe our own personal perceptions of our various real and imaginary experiences. Here are some examples:

A **PROBLEM** is...
..."a situation in need of improvement" (Parnes)
...a condition in need of change
...an unrealized goal, aim, intention or desire
...a project or task
...an unsatisfied need
...a barrier, a limitation; an obstacle to be overcome
...a constructive purpose
...an imbalance; disharmony; disorder; disunity

PROCESS is...
...a systematic sequence of steps, stages, or events
...an outline plan for managing problems and goals
...an "excursion" (Gordon)
...the path of a problem-solving journey
...a means of organizing effort and expense
...a clarification of purpose and activity

Interstellar message broadcast by the Arecibo radio telescope

METHODS are...
...ways and means; techniques; "how-tos"
...problem-solving tools
...strategies; tricks; 'trade secrets'
...sub-procedures; mini-processes

SUCCESS is...
...satisfying one's needs
...solving a problem; completing a project
...positive feedback or evaluation
...realization of achievement
...reaching one's goals...making dreams come true!

*"Products" are really **by-products** of process. If you want to increase productivity, direct your focus to procedure.*

A **CREATIVE PROBLEM-SOLVER** is...

...a self-controlled person; a "navigator"

...a behavioral self-manager

...holistic; rhythmic; alternating

...thoughtful and sensitive

...a fearless adventurer and a cautious planner

...both procedural and free-wheeling

...on-line and off-center; convergent and divergent

...a "both/and" instead of an "either/or" person

...a seeker of unique views and behaviors;

...constructive and experimental

...accepting: open-minded; relaxed; courageous

...analytic: curious; perceptive; caring

...definitive: purposive; independent; conceptual

...idea-prone: inventive; broad-minded

...decisive: assertive; self-assured; discerning

...active: persistent; determined; tireless

...evaluative: objective; critical; self-improving

...**able to behave abnormally when necessary!**

> **Note: To help yourself become more aware of your personal language (usages/definitions) for the previously listed creative problem-solving terms, take notice of the words you use when trying to explain them to others.** For example, which words would you choose as you try to explain the term "creativity" to a six-year old?...or to a close friend?...or to your parents?...or to someone with sight- and hearing-impairment? (Try explaining all of the other terms, too.)

General Travel Guides

A Book of Five Rings; Musashi, Miyamoto; Overlook Press; Woodstock, New York; 1974

A Guide to Developing Your Potential; Otto, Herbert A.; Wilshire Book Co.; N. Hollywood, CA; 1973

A Sourcebook of Creative Thinking; Parnes, Sidney, J. and Harold F. Harding; Charles Scribner's Sons; New York; 1962

Applied Imagination; Osborn, Alex; 3rd Edition; Charles Scribner's Sons; New York; 1963

Asserting Yourself; Bower, Sharon A. and Gordon H.; Addison-Wesley; Menlo Park, CA; 1991

Conceptual Blockbusting; Adams, James; 2nd Edition; W.W. Norton; New York; 1980

Creative Behavior Guidebook; Parnes, Sidney J.; Charles Scribner's Sons; New York; 1967

Developing Human Potential; a handbook; Hawley, Robert C.; ERA Press; Amherst, MA; 1975

Experiences in Visual Thinking; McKim, Robert H.; Brooks/Cole; Monterey, CA; 1972

Guide to Developing Your Potential; Otto, Herbert A.; Wilshire Book Co.; Hollywood, CA; 1973

How to Get Control of Your Time and Your Life; Lakein, Alan; David McKay Co.; New York; 1976

Imagination and Education; Egan, Kiernan; Teachers College, Columbia University; New York; 1988

In Search of Excellence; Peters, Tom J. and Robert H. Waterman, Jr.; Harper and Row, New York; 1982

Introduction to Design; Asimov, M.; Prentice-Hall; New York; 1962

Lateral Thinking; DeBono, Edward; Harper-Colophon; New York; 1973

On Becoming a Person; Rogers, Carl R.; Houghton Mifflin; Boston, MA; 1961

operating manual for spaceship earth; Fuller, R. Buckminster; Southern Illinois University Press; Carbondale, IL; 1969

Process and Reality; Whitehead, Alfred N.; Macmillan; New York; 1929

Self-Renewal; Gardner, John; Harper & Row; New York; 1963

Shifting Gears: Finding Security in a Changing World; O'Neill, George & Nena; M. Evans; New York; 1974

Swim with the Sharks without being eaten alive; McKay, Harvey; William Morrow; New York; 1988

Synectics; Gordon, William JJ; Collier/MacMillan; New York; 1961

The Amazing Brain; Ornstein, Robert E.; Houghton-Mifflin; Boston, MA; 1984

The Book of Graphic Problem-Solving; John Newcomb; R.R. Bowker; New York; 1984

The Care and Feeding of the Brain; Maguire, Jack; Doubleday; New York; 1990

The Hero Within: Six Archetypes: Six Archetypes We Live By; Pearson, Carol S.; Harper; San Francisco; 1986

The Joy of Visualization; Wells, Valerie; Chronicle Books; San Francisco; 1990

The Journal of Creative Behavior; Institute of Creative Behavior, State University of New York; Buffalo, NY; Quarterly

Quality is Free; Crosby, Philip B.; Mentor Executive Library; New York; 1979

Wishcraft: How To Get What You Really Want; Sher, Barbara with Annie Gottlieb; Ballantine; New York; 1979

Review of Part One

Before going on to become familiar with some of the many methods for improving your problem-solving adventures, why not stop to check your bearings and to review the contents of **Part One**.

Problem-solving of any variety or degree of seriousness is systematically managable when viewed as a process or sequence of logically interrelated stages or activities. Solving problems creatively, i.e., learning to be more successfully and provocatively responsive to life's challenges is largely an issue of behavioral control, not fate. Once it is understood as a **special form of human behavior, creativity** stops being one of life's mysteries, something viewed as a birthright for a privileged few which has somehow been withheld from the rest of us. Although creative behavior is indeed special behavior, it is **within reach of anyone** willing to replace old, 'normal' behaviors with new, 'abnormal', more extraordinary behaviors.

Behaviors are **methods**. The methods (behaviors) we choose to use as we progress along the paths of our problem-solving processes determine how well and how creatively our journeys will be accomplished. So-called creative people seem to be on top of every situation and able to deal 'constructively' with most of life's problems and challenges. When neccesary, they find no difficulty in behaving differently from others. How can you get to be included in that group? By gaining the required **knowledge** (becoming acquainted with procedure, methodology and related issues) and by developing the positive **attitudes** necessary for accepting challenges and seeing them to successful conclusions. It's not magic; it's simply a matter of knowing what to do, how to go about doing it, and doing it: **self-control**.

Taking charge of one's own journey through life is comparable to becoming a navigator/pilot in command of a diverse crew which is both thoughtful (left brain) and sensitive (right brain). Creative problem-solving "navigators" plan their destinations by determining the best paths from many possible paths, and control the actions of their thinking/feeling mental crew. They know that journeys which utilize all of a crew's abilities tend to be the most enjoyable and successful. **Competent 'navigators' are both rare and valuable members of society**. You can become one yourself.

DESIGN PROCESS AND THE VARIOUS CREATIVE BEHAVIORS ASSOCIATED WITH ITS SEVEN STEPS

ACCEPTING

Self-motivated; purposive; willing; accountable; dedicated; constructively discontented; trusting; concerned; loyal; enthusiatic

ANALYZING

Open-minded; lateral-thinking and vertical-thinking; curious; skeptical; subversive; sensitive; aware;; persistent; pains-taking; orderly

DEFINING

Insightful; focussed; pattern-finding; conceptual; independent; decisive; strong-willed; clear-headed

IDEA-FINDING

Option-prone; self-permissive; speculative; free-wheeling; non-judgmental; self-satisfied; inventive; fearless of originality; forward-looking; loose

SELECTING

Decisive; judgemental; fair; self-assured; assertive; self-directed; mature; discerning; logical; consistent

IMPLEMENTING

Active; constructive, communicative; expressive; managerial; resourceful; manipulative

EVALUATING

Self-educating; self-improving; critical; retrospective; introspective; prospective; self-managing.

PART TWO
MISSION CONTROL

**Choosing and Using
Various
Methods
and Techniques
for
Successful and Enjoyable
Passages through the many
Problem-Solving and
Goal-Seeking Adventures
in Life**

Welcome to **MISSION CONTROL**; the **strategic planning center** for creative problem-solving, where you'll be introduced to various ways for progressing toward your self-intended destinations. The question "what do I do now?" will no longer need to go unanswered. Instead, you will soon be reaching for the 'next step' automatically and be able to compare optional ways to head toward your destination(s) in the most satisfactory way.

Creative Problem-Solving is synonymous with design; it's an attiude; an **intentional**, purposive, process. Design involves knowing what is wanted and going for it. When you become involved with intention or design, it is assumed that you know what you're trying to achieve and that you are working on a plan for getting it. Without that, tools are meaningless. But, before seeking to acquire new and unique tools (methods), it might be good to consider the fact that having a good set of tools doesn't ensure a creative solution. It merely improves the odds for a job well done.

It's fairly certain that if you plan to develop or improve your personal creative abilities, you're going to have to allow yourself to experiment with doing things differently from time to time; to replace old, habitual ways of doing things with new, perhaps untried ways.

Methods are like recipes. Beginners follow them to the letter, whereas professionals use them as references and treat them more as guides.

Freedom to experiment with personal variations comes with experience.

Clearly reasoning that having many alternatives improves the chances for success, **creative problem-solvers** fearlessly test the effectiveness of various approaches to every task; adding all those that work for them to their permanent collection of tools. Others, without awareness of process, fear facing a large menu of options. It confuses them to have so many options. They prefer to rely on their traditional way of "always doing things (sometimes 'everything') the same way"; plowing along without considering that other approaches, although untried, might be better.

Collectively, each of the **stages** or **steps** which define a creative problem-solving process provides an overall checklist of behavioral requirements. Just as it takes practice with specific behaviors to become skilled at any stage of process, practice in learning to **alternate** between various behavioral requirements of a design process is also in order.

As you examine each separate step of the creative problem-solving process in terms of its relationship to other stages, it should become apparent that a continual variation of style between **convergent** and **divergent behavior** is involved. In one stage, you must allow yourself to remain open to all kinds of input. In another stage, often just moments later, you must wear 'blinders' and narrow your attention to but a few items. Back and forth, back and forth; open up and close down, diverge and converge, in alternating, psycho-behavioral waves throughout the entire process.

Also, as you consciously alternate between the two thinking and sensing behavioral modes in various problem and goal-seeking situations, you'll soon develop a need for more and varied tools (methods). What follows is a "starter kit" of basic problem-solving methods. By experimenting with these "tools", you'll probably devise personal variations and soon include other techniques of your own to eventually create a very personalized **'bag o -tricks'**.

Caution: Although controlled alternation between thinking and feeling may seem child-like and abnormally strange at first, it remains an important skill to re-develop if behaving more creatively is your intention...and, yes... it does require practice.

Thinking and *Taking Action* are definitely classified as **problem-solving techniques**. However, both methods are difficult to explain or improve and not always appropriate. The all-time popular problem-solving technique is usually explained as: "I don't know. I suppose I just **think** about it a lot" or "I guess I just **start working** on it."

Having such fuzzy tools for dealing with the many different kinds of tasks we face in life is extremely limiting. It's like trying to prepare specialty dishes for a gourmet meal without having the necessary kitchen equipment. Of course, it is possible to work that way. In fact, it's the way most people operate. It's just far less effective than if you have a broader range of capabilities.

In the long haul, other, more conscious techniques tend to be more effective. Some methods, because they aren't so specific are more **generally applicable** to many problem-solving types and conditions. They become **basic methods** and serve as 'universal' ways to do things. Once identifed, practiced and understood, such foundation methods simplify learning other, more specific techniques. The two most basic problem-solving methods are **List-making** and **Trial and Error**.

List-Making

Learning to generate written and drawn lists is one of the most basic and generally useful problem-solving methods to acquire. Lists allow a review of one's thinking (a left-brain activity). They also get both the left- and right-brain into the act with some conscious writing, drawing, seeing, and saying of what is felt.

List-making is an appropriate tool for a wide spectrum of tasks throughout the entire problem-solving process. The most useful variation of List-making is known as **Brainstorming** (see Ideation). which you'll soon find to be both amazingly simple to understand and a dramatically effective tool for creative problem-solving.

Trial and Error

Used consciously, **Trial and Error** (or Learn by Doing) turns the problem of "jumping to conclusions" into a learning experience. **Trial and Error** eliminates much of Analysis and Definition and jumps ahead to Implementation and Evaluation. It is often a painfully hard or expensive technique, but learning from experience can be the most appropriate way to accomplish many tasks of minimal importance.

This is undoubtedly the best method for dealing with everyday 'problems' like 'choosing ice-cream flavors for a double-dipper' at Baskin Robbins. But, it's probably not a good bet for 'deciding which car to buy,' 'which house to rent,' or for reaching important goals.

Again, conscious use of **methods won't guarantee success** just as it won't side-track your creative freedom by providing 'pat answers' or standard solutions. But, a use of **methods can help you improve your problem-solving and goal-seeking effectiveness**. You'll also develop increased personal security as you become **more accountable** for what you do and able to explain your actions to others where necessary.

The overall effectiveness of any single method/tool varies from step to step in the design process and from situation to situation in life. Therefore, each of us has our own set of preferred techniques for dealing with specific situations just as each separate stage of process also has its own, specific toolbox of generally applicable methods.

Different kinds of jobs require different kinds of tools!

Here are titles of some other basic methods for dealing with each of the seven stages of process. Can you see how they might be put to work for you?

for ACCEPTANCE (A Convergent Thinking-Feeling Stage)
Searching for Motivation; Self-Motivation; Getting Started; What's in It for Me? Make Me an Offer I can't Refuse!

for ANALYSIS (A Divergent Thinking-Feeling Stage)
What's Going on Here?; What's Involved?; Fact-Finding; Data Gathering; Questioning and Comparing

for DEFINITION (A Convergent Thinking-Feeling Stage)
Objectives-Finding; Conceptualization; Specifying Parameters; Establishing Issues and Limits; Essence-Finding; Searching for The Bottom Line

for IDEATION (A Divergent Thinking-Feeling Stage)
Ways to Win; Option-Finding; Generating Alternatives; Developing a Menu of Choices

for SELECTION (A Convergent Thinking-Feeling Stage)
Decision-Making; Comparing Options with Intentions; Finding the Best Way; Strategic Planning

for IMPLEMENTATION (A Divergent Thinking-Feeling Stage)
Making It Happen; Form-Giving; Translating Dreams into Realities; Going from Abstract to Concrete

for EVALUATION (A Convergent Thinking-Feeling Stage)
How Am I Doing?; Comparing Results with Intentions; Measuring Success; Making Plans for Improvement; Touching Base with New Expectations

One of the
amazing things about discovering
the advantages of procedure and methodology is that it's not new.
We already have experience with both topics and aren't forced to
learn them from scratch. They were there
out in front all the time !

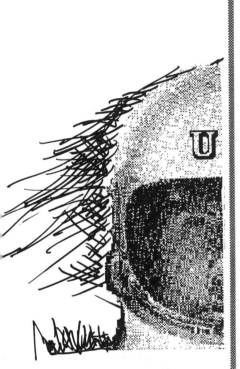

ACCEPTANCE
Convergent Thinking

ANALYSIS
Divergent Thinking

DEFINITION
Convergent Thinking

IDEATION
Divergent Thinking

IDEA-SELECTION
Convergent Thinking

IMPLEMENTATION
Divergent Thinking

EVALUATION
Convergent Thinking

The Seven Stages of Creative Problem-Solving and the Need for Alternative Thinking (and Behaving)

The First Checkpoint
on a Systematic Problem-Solving Voyage is
ACCEPTANCE

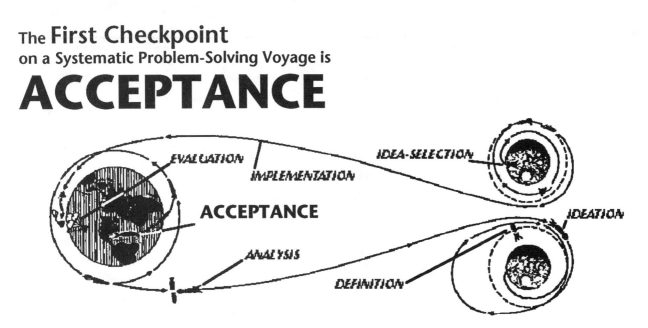

Non-creative problem-solvers, unfamilair with process, are apt to rationalize all sorts of fuzzy excuses for why they can't accept getting started on the things they say they want to do. They simply "don't know why." But, such inconclusive responses vanish with the discovery that becoming aware of the need to generate self-motivation before the fact works better than having to rely on lame excuses for failure later on. With acceptance-awareness, more personal goals get reached in more efficient and satifying ways because the impetus to continue is clear from the start.

Think about it. Isn't it true that those people who tend to be successful in reaching their goals aren't just lucky? Aren't they the same ones who knowingly accept their challenges in life? What does **self-motivation** mean after all, but **getting yourself going** and somehow **'staying with it'**?

ACCEPTANCE calls for convergent thinking. It implies a need to review personal priorities and purposes. The depth of acceptance becomes an ongoing gauge of values and commitment to the tasks involved in reaching your stated destinations. **Acceptance is synonymous with self-motivation**; it's crucial for maintaining the necessary momentum to move forward throughout an entire trip. It's like making a pact between the 'you' that wants to win and the 'you' that's got so much else to do that you can't seem to get started or keep up the pace. Aside from any external barriers outside of your control, those things inside of you which might hold you back are waiting to be identified and managed by you, the Navigator.

Acceptance is another word for motivation. When you've accepted a situation, a voyage has begun.

42

Although most of what we agree to accomplish is not life-threatening or crucial, personal goals and day-to-day problems still tend to call for a commitment somewhere in-between a casual promise and a dead-serious vow. Acceptance involves a willingness to trade energy (time, money, work) for something else (an intended goal). It's like making a contract. Agreeing to wash the dishes or take out the garbage probably won't change things too much if you don't follow through. Whereas reneging on a promise to spend four years or more working for a college degree could cause some commotion if you stopped halfway through. When the dishes and garbage bags pile up or when schoolwork starts to get shaky, your 'contracts' are put to the test.

"Broken contracts" are always a problem when other-people or some form of valuable resources are involved. Then, failure to follow through gets sticky. Applying appropriate acceptance methods at the outset of problem situations can save headaches later on. The best advice for avoiding complex acceptance problems is to **know your limits**. Getting in over your head (beyond your capabilities) or promising more than you can deliver is a major cause of disaster.

Few things require 100% commitment. Life is more forgiving than that. You probably couldn't feasibly give 100% even if you promised to do so. The Marine Corps' demand for **"110%"** from its recruits is merely a provocative way of saying they will accept nothing less than complete attention to duty. The real issue is how well you understand the fact that your depth of involvement is also **a measure of your commitment**. In short, you tend to 'get what you pay for.' If you want successful results, you've got to willingly invest enough of yourself to succeed.

Be cautious of biting off more than you can chew. It's easy to rush into a situation, but often difficult to back out of one.

Language Guide
To Accept a Problem Situation is..

.. to commit your energies to an aim or goal
.. to establish motives and become motivated
.. to get started and keep moving
.. to revise existing priorities
.. to decide to make a dream come true
.. to assume responsibility for realizing an intention
.. to agree; contract; sign a pact
.. to take on another 'passenger'

Methods for
Acceptance

Alternative Ways to
Get Started and Stay Involved

This section of **Mission Control** contains a variety of techniques for creatively **taking charge** of a problem-solving process from the outset. As you examine this menu of ways to get started and keep going, try to determine which one or ones might fit best into your personal plans and situations. (NOTE: If a method seems O.K., but the name doesn't suit you, try changing its title to something more to your liking.)

1. WHAT'S IN IT FOR ME?
2. MAKING ROOM (Personal Priorities)
3. GO-GETTER
4. WHO'S IN CHARGE, ANYWAY?
5. MISSION IMPOSSIBLE
6. GIVE IT UP: A TRAGIC SCENARIO
7. SUCCESS, AT FIRST !
8. ROLE MODEL
9. CON MAN (Contingency Management)
10. DECLARATION OF ACCEPTANCE
11. AMBIVALENCE
12. STANISLAVSKI
13. CARPE DIEM !
14. BLOCKBUSTING
15. THE PROFESSIONAL

The effectiveness of any method is measured by how well it is suited to the situation at hand.

WHAT'S IN IT FOR ME?

It's easier to 'get up and go' if you know ahead of time what you'll derive from all your efforts, i.e., what the payoff's going to be somewhere down the line.

Try **listing the benefits** you might accrue if you become involved in your project. This often works to help break yourself loose from the satisfaction of *status quo* and get you moving toward those expected rewards.

MAKING ROOM (Personal Priorities)

Any task is easier to accept if you can clearly see that there is room to include it in your current schedule. If you are prone to "bite off more than you can (or are willing to) chew," you can avoid this self-made stressful condition by identifying your priorities, checking to see if there actually is sufficient space to fit another 'project' into your life, and clearly deciding that the new activity you are proposing is truly superior to what currently occupies that time/energy slot.

The method involves a) charting your current hourly/ weekly time schedule by showing **all current commitments**, b) estimating the **time and energy requirements** for the new project, and c) determining how the two might converge. When your plans and your schedule fit together, acceptance comes easily.

GO-GETTER

Belief in the admonition **"you get what you pay for"** keeps many people actively involved in working hard to get what they want from life. It provides a kind of built-in **self-starter**. For go-getters, the problem of accepting a task is academic. It makes little difference to them who or what "pushes their button" with a challenge. Once pushed, they're automatically up and going. They seem to value challenge and the activity of the problem-solving process more than the resolution. They tend to enjoy the day-to-day living of life rather than only the rare moments of success experienced along the way . Why not try it yourself?

WHO'S IN CHARGE, ANYWAY?

This method is a test of self-control or how well you are able to manage your thinking and your behavior. It is based on the fact that the sooner you can teach your ego to play along with your id, the quicker you'll be able to push yourself to get started and help yourself to keep moving.

45

Remember: Your left brain regulates thinking and your right brain controls doing. When you're "navigating", you're in charge of both your thinking and your doing. The real secret is to teach each side of your brain to play along with the other side.

MISSION IMPOSSIBLE

If you want to simplify getting involved in solving a problem or reaching a goal, try thinking of the problem/project as something adventurous and exciting. When you feel the adrenaline rushing through your veins, it will be difficult to hold you back.

The old TV adventure series, *Mission Impossible*, accentuated acceptance with each of its weekly problem situations. The opening line qualifier, "Your mission, **should you choose to accept it**, is...," left no doubts in the minds of its viewers that once an assignment was accepted it would be resolved in an interesting, exciting way. Perhaps the adventurer in you needs a similar challenge to incite the otherwise more cautious you to depart on an exciting 'secret mission' of your own.

GIVE IT UP: A TRAGIC SCENARIO

What might happen if you did not accept the situation in question? Would it make a big difference in your life? or none at all? Who would care? What terrible things might occur? Would it cost you dearly? Think about it: what would be lost if you stopped worrying about it right now and just went back to what you were doing before? It's just possible that running through these scenarios could either save you a lot of wasted energy or help you find an important reason for breaking the inertia and becoming motivated.

For example: A member of a car pool, afraid of failure and unwilling to take a driver's license test, might benefit from playing out the embarassing scenario of explaining their childish condition to other members of the pool. The unpleasant fantasy may be enough to eliminate the fear and motivate them to take the test.

SUCCESS, AT FIRST!

One sure-fire way to get off to a running start is to jump over all the hard work and begin at the end. By envisioning yourself as having done your very best and already enjoying the satisfaction of your efforts, you can use your imagination to create a convincing picture of success.

The 'positive' psychology of seeing yourself winning before the race has even started can serve as an energizer; not just to get you started, but also, as a beneficial booster to help out all the way to the finish line.

In terms of the problem or project which confronts you, ask yourself what would it be like to really succeed. How would winning make you feel? How differently might you be treated by your family, pals, mentors? What 'awards' or rewards would you receive?

An important thing to remember, if this method is to work for you, is to **stay positive** by imagining success in the most pleasurable terms you can invent.

ROLE-MODEL

Having a role-model as a guide can often become the easiest way to stimulate self-motivation. Just being around people who readily accept the challenges in their lives can be an excellent, simple way to break down your own reticence and get you going.

People who readily accept challenges aren't the only 'models' which might be helpful. Other things which 'accept' can also serve as guides for eliminating personal barriers. For example: a first-class toaster accepts a variety of types and sizes of bread, English muffins, waffles, etc. It does so by providing a large, deep receiving chamber, a simply-operated push-bar, twin heating elements and a programmable timer. Mediocre toasters, on the other hand, tend to lack those necessary qualities to perform well. The 'lessons' of the toaster might also be applied to you.

CON MAN (Contingency Management)

'**Contingencies**', whether real or imaginary, will always be in the way of progress; i.e., things which often seem "outside of our control"; sub-problems which have to be resolved before we can begin working on our primary projects. "It's not my fault," we might say, "I just can't seem to get started because such and such is in my way." 'sound familiar?

Behavioral psychology comes to the rescue by offering **four easy-to-follow rules** for managing the contingencies in our lives. Collectively called "behavior modification," the guidelines are simply stated as:

1. **UNDERSTAND YOUR LIMITS.** You can only do so much and no more. Don't fool yourself by imagining you can become far more capable overnight.

2. **ESTABLISH FEASIBLE GOALS** and reasonable standards for what you're trying to achieve. Bring your intentions into balance with your abilities.

3. **BE STRICT and CONSISTENT.** Refuse to allow any exception to 'reasonable, feasible' standards.

4. **REWARD YOURSELF** for "good" behavior (and/or punish yourself for being "bad"). Provide some real incentives (or deterrents), not just empty promises. Some reluctant creatures are encouraged to move forward with offers of 'carrots'; others require brow-beating with 'sticks'. Perhaps one (or both) is for you?

Knowing the limits of your personal "fabric" allows you to plan how it might be stretched without being torn.

DECLARATION OF ACCEPTANCE

If your basic fear of punishment (the 'stick') works best to get you going, it's possible that you might capitalize on another normal human fear. For instance, some people just can't make headway until they feel some intimidating pressure from people they respect.

To create your own pressure, set yourself up to look really bad if you fail. Make your intentions and goals clear to everyone around you by using some form of written or often repeated declaration. When everyone is familiar with your proposed plan, it becomes a matter of either 'doing it' or suffering the painful ridicule of friends. It's childish, but it might work. Try displaying your written declaration as a poster in a prominant place, or mailing xerox copies to those whose respect you cherish.

11 AMBIVALENCE

There are probably many interrelated factors involved with reluctance and reticence. It's not unusual to find a combination of such reasons relating to specific instances of non-acceptance. Managing these 'hang-ups' is easier if we know what's really behind them and how that background relates to our unwillingness to get started. One common culprit is **ambivalence** or **conflicting values**.

Ambivalence is usually a simple matter of old values not yet caught up to agreeing with new aspirations. A typical example occurs when the desire to be innovative meets the need for approval by one's peers. The new intention requires adventure and risk, yet the peers (seem to) demand caution and conformity; an apparent stalemate.

Getting to know more about what we believe (our values) and therefore what we have a tendency to respect in life is always beneficial to self-management.

12 STANISLAVSKI

The famous Russian dramatic coach and theatrical director, Constantin Stanislavski, was best noted for his contribution known as **method acting**. The principles he formulated provide choice advice to those desirous of becoming more involved in what they do. Stanislavski's rules help guide theatrical stars to accept their assigned roles. If Brando could 'beome the part,' perhaps you can too.

Stanislavski writes of being "ceremonious" and turning tasks into more memorable events by treating them with "reverence and respect." He suggests a necessity for a kind of **love affair** with the **magical** or **mystical qualities** of the task and a kind of light-headed and **buoyant relationship** with it. He refers to the need to **flow with it** and to **allow it to carry you** (giving up of yourself in order to become more like it) instead of confronting it or trying to control it.

He suggests the need to drop all preconceptions and general opinions about the situation in order to meet it with an open mind and a welcoming heart.

13   CARPE DIEM!

There's nothing quite as positive as people with a purpose; a reason to live and to enjoy life. They seem to love what they do. And, they tend to do it well because of the clear connection they make between purpose, process, and product. Psychologist Abraham Maslov referred to that type of person as being **"self-actualized"**; as having reached the stage of enjoying 'inner peace'; as having a relaxed feeling of oneness with nature.

Once you believe that what you do is valid and has meaning and purpose and you decide to see yourself as a constructive problem-solver open to dealing with any dilemma which attracts your interest, then reluctance to accept the conditions of any particular situation should cease to exist.

Hard work does not guarantee success. But, diligence does improve the odds for winning in any endeavor.

14   BLOCKBUSTING

Change may be exciting, but it is **rarely comfortable**. Change necessitates re-adapting to new conditions. This means added work to regain self-control. The natural tendency, therefore, is to resist change and stay put. By the time we reach adulthood, we've generally become very good at resisting change and the extra stress it causes by creating a variety of "blocks" to retain our status quo.

Exploding such barriers to the changes which accompany productivity is a full-time job for creative problem-solvers who are eager to get to the real meat of their challenges without being held back by their natural tendencies. Instead of waiting for inspiration, they work to identify and resolve their psychological blocks by considering changes in their lives as productive adventures rather than as threats to security.

15 THE PROFESSIONAL

There's a lot to be said in favor of moving up from amateur status to professional standing. It's not too different from "**growing up**," i.e., leaving the uncertainties of childhood behind and beginning to behave responsibly.

Professional behavior brings together all that is positive and **accountable**. Society depends on its professionals (and writes laws to ensure that professional behavior meets above average performance standards). Professionals accept many tasks that others "wouldn't touch." They are hard-working and diligent, not because they must, but because they have decided to do their best toward maintaining the respect of those they serve. It's **a way of life**, a matter of **self-respect**, rather than a "job".

Guidebooks for
Acceptance

Conceptual Blockbusting; Adams, James; W.W. Norton Co.; New York; 1980

Developing Attitude Toward Learning; Mager, Robert; Fearon; Belmont, CA; 1968

Does it Matter?; Watts, Alan; Vintage Press; New York; 1971

Motivation and Personality; Maslow, A.H.; Harper; New York; 1954

The Second Stage on a
Systematic Problem-Solving Voyage is

ANALYSIS

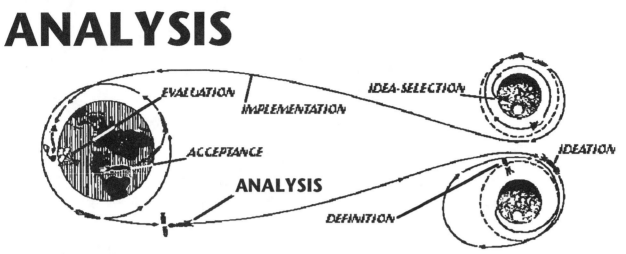

Analysis is a divergent thinking, 'legwork' step of the creative problem-solving process. It's the stage of un-covering and discovering what you'll need to know to intelligently "home-in" on your destination or goal and to effectively deal with its problems. It's a time for **gathering facts** and for examining how all the collect-ed data fits together.

You should note that the **Analysis** stage is also a **test** of having passed the **Acceptance** stage. If the task of find-ing the information you'll need to go on bothers you, you can bet that Acceptance still needs your attention.

When situations are serious and more responsible be-havior is in order, it's certainly wise to become deeply informed on a subject or situation before taking action to change it. But, there is a great natural temptation to leap right over Analysis and go directly to Idea-finding or beyond. Actually, that shorthand approach works ef-fectively in simple, relatively unimportant day-to-day situations where ignorance of facts isn't a serious short-coming. Then there are other times when the amount and quality of information requried for dealing crea-tively with a situation depends on both your skill in data-gathering and your degree of commitment.

"Tough problems" (the ones which seem to be either complex or hard to unravel...or both) are also the ones less likely to be accepted and analyzed. This common dilemma is best resolved via self-awareness and situa-tional fact-finding. The more you know about both the problem and why you're holding back, the sooner you can get on with the work required to move forward. It's somewhat of a vicious circle, i.e., you can't go on

Ignorance implies a lack of knowledge. There are no "ignorant questions"; only ignorant people.

until you're already up and going. Remember: A positive viewpoint can quickly change any resistance to fact-finding into part of an enjoyable journey.

Since serious or important issues often require tediously long periods of fact-finding research, the result often leaves a false impression that all forms of research are potentially endless and boring. On the contrary, most simple situations require little or no research beyond what you already know. Research only tends to be boring when the researcher is uninterested in the subject or when a single source of knowledge has been squeezed dry.

To break the spell of staring into only one information source, it may help to consider a wider variety of sources and methods. Ecology shows that some relationship can be found between all things, i.e., **'all things are interrelated.'** This basic fact implies that information exists everywhere and that to uncover a spectrum of data about anything, it's generally wise to **look into more than one place** for facts.

However, searching for information can easily become endless; especially if the amount of energy spent for Analysis is left undetermined. And, since there is always more to learn and discover about everything, Analysis files should always remain open.

Knowing when it's time to stop adding new information can be best determined by establishing a fact-finding deadline. Dont forget that there will always be other opportunities for digging up more data later on...as you solve other problems and seek new goals throughout life.

Language Guide
To Analyze a Problem Situation is..

.. to become involved in fact-finding
.. to research the subject or situation
.. to question and compare
.. to gather data or information
.. to look inside the problem; search for insight
.. to examine, dissect, decompose the situation
.. to become familiar or friendly with the problem

53

Methods for
Analysis

Alternative Ways
for Gathering Information
about a Goal or Problem Situation

Creative problem-solvers always **consider the facts** before "sticking their necks out." If you have an urge to jump over all of the "hard work" of digging up the pertinent questions and related facts and to rush ahead with ready-made answers, it's no more than a normal reaction. But, try to remember that, although fearlessness and daring can serve you well as a creative problem-solver, being bullishly headstrong and/or avoiding important information are definitely not creative behaviors.

Since all problem-solving journeys are unique adventures, the relative usefulness of the following methods will vary depending on their relevance to your personality and changing needs.

1. SENSITIVITY AND COMMON SENSE
2. MICRO-MACRO
3. IDEA-DUMP
4. TRAVELER'S JOURNAL
5. LOOK IT UP
6. THE PACKRAT AND THE COLLECTOR
7. FORCE-FIT
8. ATTRIBUTE LISTING
9. BACK TO THE SUN
10. LATERAL THINKING
11. MODEL-MAKER
12. UNDER A ROCK; IN THE CORNER
13. MORPHOLOGY
14. PATTERNS AND PARADIGMS
15. SQUEEZE IT AND STRETCH IT
16. JUMPING TO CONCLUSIONS

SENSITIVITY AND COMMON SENSE

A simple, direct way to get information is to ask questions about anything or anyone you suspect might be related to the situation. Start by asking yourself.

Begin your analysis by clearing your mind of all that you already know about the issues. You'll be amazed to learn how much you actually do know about your subject without looking it up. You can **listen to yourself think** by talking about the problem. You can **see yourself think** by writing about the problem and making sketches of your thoughts. Plus, you can **feel yourself think** by becoming aware of the vibrations you create when talking about the problem. To increase your sensitivity to a situation, try getting several of your senses working together "in common."

For various reasons, this fundamental method is often put off until later (sometimes too late) on the assumption that it will only yield 'the obvious.' Instead of beginning with more complex ways for acquiring information, train yourself to **speak up** for information early in the game and to **write down** your responses. If what you produce is really no more than "obvious", at least that much is clearly 'out in front' and won't have to be rediscovered later on.

Questions breed answers. Ask and you shall receive. There are no stupid questions. But, it is stupid not to ask for answers when you need them.

MICRO-MACRO

Insight and **"outsight"** represent two different vistas: a micro-view and a macro-view. As children, we develop our insights by getting as close to things as possible. We touch, taste, listen to, and smell everything. As we age, we get more and more distant from things and learn to stand apart from them in order to better see the external relationships between things instead of more information about the things themselves. Big pictures and overall patterns are easier to spot from the outside.

Although the normal adult approach to life is to maintain some protective distance from things, a creative analysis includes both up-close and overall views. Anyone knows that you can't discover much about what's inside of something by only standing outside of it.

55

IDEA DUMP

Instead of relaxing in the satisfaction that you already have the answers and need no further research, stop to jot down any or all of those ready-made solutions. Not only will you be able to see much of your related knowledge at a glance, you'll also become aware of what you don't yet know, freeing yourself to seek deeper insight in the process.

If you already have a solution, you'll find little incentive to search for information leading to another solution. A variation of the previous method, this technique involves cleansing the mind of ready answers. By 'laying all your cards on the table,' you'll be better able to view and address the critical issues of any preconception and to better deal with the otherwise non-creative and close-minded "Don't bother me with facts; I've got my mind made up" sort of attitude which stops many problem-solvers.

TRAVELER'S JOURNAL

Creative travelers rarely embark on a journey without having referred to journals published by previous travelers. To them, "don't leave home without it" means 'remembering to pack a fresh journal' of their own. Keeping a logbook or journal of your voyage not only allows you to remember your discoveries, it also provides a way to keep all your facts together. If your project is an important one, a journal can become its orderly and organizing workplace. Although becoming more popular, journal-keeping is still considered to be a creative behavior since 'normal' people are generally too busy worrying about their projects to deal with them so rigorously.

When you can see your thoughts you are able to edit and improve them. With a graphic record of what crossed your mind, you can quickly recall and update what you were thinking yesterday or last week or even a few minutes ago; something not generally possible if you merely try keeping your thoughts "in your head."

This documentary method (derived form the Italian 'giorno' for 'day') involves "keeping a journal" or daily record. Aside from being appropriate for the Analysis stage, journal-keeping lends itself to all stages of a goal-seeking or problem-solving process by serving as a portable file cabinet and permanent record for a project. Many varieties of notebooks and 'blank books' are available for applying this method to your project.

LOOK IT UP

Although the problem-solving or goal-seeking paths you travel may seem to be uniquely special, it's highly probable that other 'travelers' have experienced similar joys and pitfalls before you. Learning from the experience of previous problem-solvers, instead of having to re-discover the same things over and over again, is not only an energy-saving method; it is also a significant creative behavior. Your perspective can become much more far-ranging when you are "standing on the shoulders of giants."

Ask any intelligent student how to find information and you'll be advised to "look it up." It seems overly obvious, but most people forget to try this well-known and basic analytic method. A modern library is the best overall resource for discovering what past "experts" discovered about things which now concern you. Reference Room librarians and computerized information retrieval systems you'll find there can quickly put you in touch with much of the recorded wisdom that has preceded you.

Reference books abound on every subject. They're just not always sitting on a table in front of you. One has to make an effort to go to the bookshelf or to the library or to where ever help might be located. Dictionaries, encyclopediae, magazines and journals, reports, data banks, information retrieval systems and electronic networks; all await your request for data.

If you find that you are unable to get to a source of information physically, use a telephone to speed you there. The amount of facts you can get by spending an hour or two gathering the data you need electronically is amazing. All major university and public libraries worldwide are linked by computerized networks with minimal cost for facsimile reproduction.

THE PACKRAT AND THE COLLECTOR

The difference between a "packrat" and a "collector" is that packrats accumulate piles of stuff. Although, much of what they gather is useless, they enjoy being able to select what they need when they need it from the pile of miscellany. Collectors, on the other hand, sort-out only the material which they deem appropriate as they progress. Both gathering styles have benefits and limitations: packrats waste lots of energy and need to be a bit more discriminating, while collectors miss some potentially important opportunities and need to have more open minds.

You might enjoy a change of pace by playing one or both of these "gatherer" roles when seeking the information you need to reach your goal or to solve a problem. Plus, because you can start off with an awareness of their separate shortcomings, you can be far more efficient than either one by striking a balance between their often limited performances.

FORCE-FIT

Harmony and Contrast, two fundamental design principles derived from observing nature, help us realize that all things are both alike and different from everything else; that both similarities and differences exist between all things. By comparing your problem subject with other subjects, you can use the 'harmony/contrast' principle as a method for uncovering all sorts of previously passed-over information about it.

Be cautious of making overly obvious comparisons, like comparing automobiles with buses, which will only produce more of what you already know. Truly unique information, by definition, comes from taking a unique viewpoint, i.e., looking beyond and beneath the surfaces of things. If you want to discover deeper realizations, you'll have to **stretch** your limits and compare truly different things: like comparing an automobile with spaghetti or with Easter or computer software, instead of with something so similar as a bus.

58

ATTRIBUTE LISTING

Normally, we get to know someone or something better, piece-by-piece and over extended periods of time. We slowly gather information until we know the complete spectrum of their attributes; those characteristics that make them who and what they are.

Attribute listing is easiest when you **begin with general categories and work your way down to specifics**. For example, when fact-finding about a problem dealing with locating a job overseas, you might begin with general categories, such as: Personal Qualifications and Limitations; Expected Benefits; Estimated Costs; Consultants; etc. Then go on to list specific details under each of those headings in order to generate more complete lists of related facts. Items listed under 'Costs', for instance, might be: Overseas Travel Options, Living Costs, Insurance, Wardrobe Requirements, Foreign Language Courses, etc.

If done systematically, lengthy lists of attributes quickly generated with only moderate costs of time and effort, can encompass the 'world' of any person or subject. Where such lists become overly complex or detailed, the items can be compared, ranked, and prioritized to help in managing them more efficiently, or they might be sub-divided into smaller sub-lists.

Remember: Those who are ignorant of history are often "condemned" to repeat it.

BACK TO THE SUN

Much of what we want to know about in life is physical. When seeking to make a physical improvement, it makes little sense to venture into dealing with the fuzzier level of abstractions before establishing a solid base in physical reality. This simple and direct analysis technique can help form a perspective of the physical data of any subject quickly. It evolves from the fact that all physical things are eventually reducible to solar energy, our biosphere's primary physical support system. An indirect, added benefit of this method dealing with the chain of physical interrelationships is its potential for increasing basic environmental design conciousness.

The technique works this way: First, list the basic or component parts of your subject. Then, in a series of steps, reduce each component to its previous subsequent levels of development from its solar origin.

Example: In dealing with a problem involving sports injuries, you may need to analyze a **running shoe**. The list of **basic physical components** for the shoe in question might include: A. Plastic Sole with Synthetic Rubber Inserts; B. Plastic Upper Reinforcements; C. Nylon Fabric Upper; D. Cotton Fabric Padding and Lining; E. Cotton Laces;F. Painted Steel Grommets; G. Decorative Plastic Appliques; H. I. Nylon Thread; J. Plastic Adhesives; etc.. In turn, each separate basic component might be then **reduced sequentially** as follows: A. Plastic Sole: Steel Molds, Chemical Dyes, Plastic Adhesives, Chemical/ Petroleum Synthetics, Polymers, Crude Oil, Decayed Vegetation, Water, and finally, Solar Energy. B. Plastic/ Fabric Upper: Nylon Fabric; Poly-plastic Sheet; Nylon Thread, etc. Reducing each of these one by one, still one step further; as Steel Molds: Clay or Wax Form Model, Sand Casting, Molten Metal, etc. The list lengthens quickly with each level of depth.

LATERAL THINKING

In the overall context of nature, **all things are interrelated**. Ideally, a complete folio of analytic findings for any specific subject contains the combined information from both **close-up** scrutiny and **wide-angle** overview. By thinking "laterally" across many subjects, instead of merely "vertically" within a single subject, previously unseen (unique) connections become more evident.

This wide-angle technique is a 'tag-on' to a method for increasing creative awareness introduced by the British author/lecturer, Edward DeBono. It follows the principle that discovery is more likely to result from a macro- or **broad view** approach of seeking relationships between different subjects than via a micro-approach of only digging deeper within the bounds of the subject.

Instead of allowing yourself to go 'stale' by "digging the same hole deeper," try branching out to include different kinds of connections with other, apparently 'unrelated', subjects. Perhaps this method can help you see many 'other' relationships that previously went unnoticed, but were right there in front of you all along.

*Aside from definitive
small scale versions of objects,
models come in a wide variety of
verbal, behavioral, and visual
two- and three-dimensional forms;
such as charts, graphs, diagrams,
drawings, scenarios, and games
of a variety of kinds.*

*"All things are inter-related.
We are all alike. Everything
is the same thing."*
Ancient Zen Proverb

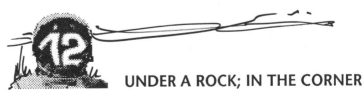

11 MODEL-MAKER

'Insightful' information about almost any subject can be found via modeling, i.e., abstractly simulating or representing the real thing. Combined with an active imagination, models provide an efficient, although still somewhat vicarious means for experiencing the objects, places, and situations which are not financially feasible to examine in real-time or at full-size.

Models are cost-effective ways to examine a subject from different points of view. Compared to real physical testing, models cost very little in terms of the overall time and energy they can save. Gathering analytical data from a physical or verbal model simulation, instead of only from real experiences learned at 'the school of hard knocks,' is clearly a creative behavior.

Small, handmade three-dimensional simulations of functional, environmental, or architectural designs are commonly known examples of how large, expensive, complex objects and environmental settings can be studied before full-size construction begins. But, other two-dimensional forms of modeling spaces and places can be equally effective, such as **relationship chart**s and **'bubble'** diagrams indicating organizational, functional, structural or environmental connections: **computer-simulations** in the form of 'walk-throughs' of spatial sequences and 'view-arounds' of 3-D forms; detailed narrative descriptions; expressionistic abstractions; games; etc. Verbal metaphors, which allow the study of one subject by examining another subject, are simple, useful forms of modeling.

12 UNDER A ROCK; IN THE CORNER

Information exists everywhere; not just in the "obvious" places. If you reach an analysis dead-end, try some of the not-so-obvious sources; places you wouldn't normally look. In the library for example, after perusing the directly-related materials on your subject, stop to take a peek at some 'other' "unrelated" areas. If the subject is children, try the aeronautics, chemical engineering, or cooking sections.

MORPHOLOGY

The scientific analysis of structure and form involves **sub-dividing wholes into parts** or constituent categories and components. The method is known as **morphological analysis**; a process of breaking large, complex entities into ever-smaller, more manageable, 'bite-size' pieces.

Morphologies are commonly expressed in terms of two- and three-dimensional charts where primary categories are represented by the major axes with smaller subdivisions shown as 'cells' within those axes. When examined systematically, every detail of a subject can be painstakingly studied in terms of its relationship to every other detail until all of the sub-relationships have been examined. It's long-winded, but far-reaching, and essential to serious research.

A classic example is the morphological chart used to examine education in terms of teaching and learning. The three 'faces' of an X-Y-Z chart are used to represent the traditional educational and behavioral "learning domains": the **cognitive** (factual) **domain**, the **psycho-motor** (physical control, skills) **domain**, and the **affective** (values and beliefs) **domain**. Sub-categories within each domain are then made to interact with the sub-categories of the other two domains in XY, XZ, and XYZ relationships until all 'cell' interelationships are examined.

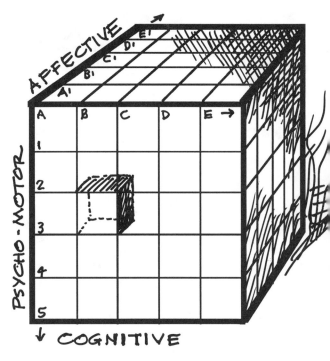

A fringe benefit from use of the Morphological Analysis technique, aside from its help in analysis by providing of view of the total 'realm' of a subject, is its ability to point out 'holes' of missing information in a research project. If you're looking for a 'unique' project in any interest area, this is one sure way to find it.

PATTERNS AND PARADIGMS

Because patterns can be found and identified in all problem-solving and goal-seeking situations, pattern-seeking is a generic method for becoming acquainted with any subject.

Patterns are **repetitions**. There are many forms of repetition: time, distance, quantity, quality, event, color, texture, behavior, name, etc. Some patterns are clearly observable; others are more obscure. We search for patterns in life because they help us to understand, recognize and remember people, things and events. **Paradigms** are the conclusions drawn from a pattern or a set of patterns. Paradigms are similar to **analogies**; both are based on **observed patterns**. Paradigms are used for applying something learned from one set of patterns when dealing with other real or potential patterns.

The basic principles of physics and life sciences, for example, are paradigms derived from observing repetitions and patterns in nature. Those observed natural patterns deemed most important become "laws" to "live by." From observing seasonal cycles on growth and behavior, we learn to distinguish positive and negative effects of natural contrasts and balances. The positive part then becomes a paradigm or guide for dealing with other types of cyclical events in our own lives. Another example is shown by how we learn to be cautious of over-indulgence by noticing the pattern wherein most forms of natural excess are typically compensated by conservation, illness, and/or disease.

SQUEEZE IT AND STRETCH IT

When managed creatively, the multi-stage problem-solving (design) process requires using both brain functions (thinking and behaving) as well as using those functions to alternate freely between each of the two divergent and convergent modes. Creative designers learn to control their switching back and forth between those two complementary activities. At one stage, they must broaden their horizons to include as many details as possible; at another stage, compressing much information and many alternatives into a select few.

Such "squeezing and stretching" of subject content allows information to be quickly collected, while simultaneously broadening the spectrum of possibilities. After piles of data are gathered, it can then be digested into more compact observations.

'Stretching' a subject requires asking a series of "what?" **questions** and providing the answers. To 'squeeze' a subject, a series of **"why?" questions** and responses is needed. Asked in an alternating pattern of whats and whys, such questions you get closer and closer to knowing what a subject is all about...or at least to revealing what you still need to learn about it.

Example problem: **I'll need extra money if I really want to have that dreamed-of summer vacation in Spain. How can I get it?**

Q. (Stretch) **What** do I need money for?

A. Airline fare, car rental, hotels, new clothes, etc.

Q. (Squeeze) **Why** must I fly, stay in hotels and buy new clothes?

A. It's faster, ..more private, ..good for my morale,...

Q. (Stretch) **What's** the purpose of taking this trip?

A. To relax, see new places, have new experiences.

Q. (Squeeze) **Why** do you need to relax, etc.?

A. My job is starting to wear me down and I've lost interest in what I'm doing.

Q. (Stretch) **What** can travel do to correct the problem?

A. It can help me recharge my interest in... etc.

JUMPING TO CONCLUSIONS

Finally, don't forget the ever-popular method of analysis familiar to everyone as "trial and error." Although it can be costly, sometimes the quickest and best way to find out about something is to try it out. In everyday (normal) situations, this technique is used largely by default without consciousness of the fact that other options might be better suited to the task. The result is that the lessons learned from most of life's analysis are dearly paid for with buckets of blood, sweat, and tears.

Jumping To Conclusions is clearly not the best-suited analysis method when designing a skyscraper, but it's certainly not a bad choice when you need to discover how to gain a favor from a friend or how to write a 'letter to the editor' or other, not so dramatically important situations.

Guidebooks for
Analysis

Analyzing Performance Problems; Mager, Robert; Fearon; Belmont, CA; 1970

Born Curious; Hodgkin, R.A.; Wiley; New York and London; 1976

Design Methods, Jones, J. Christopher; Wiley-Interscience; London; 1970

Goal Analysis; Mager, Robert; Fearon; Belmont, CA; 1972

Learning: Analysis and Application; Travers, John F.; D. McKay Co.; New York; 1972

Modelbuilder's Notebook; Moore, Fuller; McGraw-Hill; New York, etc.; 1990

Multiple Factor Analysis; Thurstone, Louis L.; University of Chicago Press; Chicago; 1947

Research Without Copying; Polette, Nancy; Book Lures; O'Fallon, MO; 1988

Stanislavski's Legacy; Stanislavski, Konstantin & Elizabeth Reynolds; Theatre Arts Books; New York; 1968

Synectics, Gordon, William J.J.; Harper & Row; New York; 1966

The **Third Stage** on a
Systematic Problem-Solving Voyage is
Definition

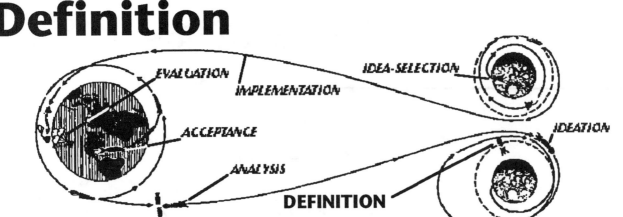

Definitions provide the directional bearings needed for creative problem-solving voyages. They set the compass for success. They provide a clear picture of where you're headed. The **Definition** stage is a time for translating the discoveries of Analysis into meaning and direction. Whereas Analysis was a divergent thinking stage of gathering lots of data from many corners, Definition is a period of **convergent thinking**; a time for digesting data in order to discover its essential parts. To define is to "boil down" or "distill" information.

Definition is the **link** between **Analysis** and **Synthesis**. It's an encapsulation of a problem situation; an expression of intention and/or expectation. In a nutshell, to **define** something is to establish its essential **meaning**.

Definition clarifies process by highlighting its crucial content. We **derive** definitions **from Analysis** and we **apply** them **to Synthesis**. Awareness of a problem's definition or meaning marks the big difference between professional problem-solvers and those who simply 'feel their way'; not really knowing quite where they're headed or what they're trying to achieve.

Creative people seem to "see things differently" from others, not because of a magical gift of insight, but mainly because they stop to analyze situations and determine meanings instead of rushing headlong into reactionary conclusions. It's far more normal to refer to problems superficially, such as "This job drives me nuts...I'm quiting!" instead of procedurally as "I've got to find out what's wrong with this job and start to deal with that."

Normal behavior is reactionary, not definition-seeking behavior. It's normal to repeat mistakes by reacting to

In theory, once you know where you're headed, you're already half-way there.

> *Creative problem-solvers meet obstacles in their path like everyone else. But, being unsure of where they're headed isn't one of them. They know that there are many paths to every goal.*

> *Where problems aren't clearly stated and goals remain obscure, resolutions and conclusions tend to be equally fuzzy.*

life's varied stimuli sub-consciously, without learning from previous experiences. But, awareness of the need for identifying the essence of problem and goal situations changes all that.

We derive personal meaning (definition) from our experiences through the screens of our individual perceptions. The result is that each of us has a personal **point-of-view** about everything, and consequently the spectrum of meanings is wide. Some of our viewpoints are conscious and clear; some of them are subconscious and foggy. Some of them are profound; some superficial or mundane. Some are poetic; others are crude; some constructive; others destructive. As more and more meanings accrue, we tend to formulate a set of behavioral rules, or personal **values**, from them. Awareness of experience and the values we derive from it allows us to become more in charge of our actions. In the process, our understanding of life expands and new insights develop.

A collection of the various meanings that people have assigned to their experiences can be found in any unabridged dictionary. But, dictionaries don't contain absolute meanings, merely collections of various usages (other people's definitions). So-called **"true meanings" are relative** to particular people and situations. If you try to find a commonly agreed-upon meaning for the expression 'a good time,' for example, you'll soon see the search as a near-impossible task. No reference exists for absolute or essential meanings for things so subjective. In the end, we must either **derive our meanings from personal experience** or **accept the definitions of others**. Most of us use a combination of both options.

Language Guide
To DEFINE a Problem Situation is..

...to extract its essential meaning
...to express its key ingredient(s)
...to determine a meaningful connection between Analysis and Synthesis
...to find direction; to establish bearing
...to clarify objectives or expectations
...to get to the heart of the matter
...to reveal the crux, the core, the truth!
...to establish the criteria for a happy ending
...**to specify the standards for success!**

Methods for
Definition

Alternative Ways
for Clarifying Directions
in Problem-Solving or Goal-Seeking

Having a definition provides a 'handle' on the situation; a way of grabbing onto what's really involved; knowledge of where you're really headed. Here is a selection of techniques for breaking through the confusing outer crust of problem-solving/goal-seeking situations.

The difficulty here is not so much related to finding definitions, because meanings are numerous and varied, but in selecting that single meaning which feels good enough to live with for the duration of a particular problem-solving journey. Although you are seeking essential meaning(s), beware that the word 'essential' need not imply earth-shaking, innovative, or uniquely creative. Those qualities can come later on in the more expressive stages of Synthesis when meanings get translated into formalized concrete terms. Simple, direct viewpoints often have a better chance of being developed into creatively unique solutions than do ones which are exotic, overly complex, forced, or hard to explain.

Remember: GIGO!
(Garbage In; Garbage Out!)
The quality of a definition is closely related to the depth and extent of analysis.

1. **PARAPHRASED CONNECTIONS**
2. **PRIORITIES**
3. **TALK IT OUT; WRITE IT OUT**
4. **KEY WORDS**
5. **SYNECTICS**
6. **RECIPES AND FORMULAE**
7. **PROBLEMS WITHIN PROBLEMS**
8. **BOIL IT DOWN (Essence-Finding)**
9. **MISSION OBJECTIVE(S)**
10. **CROSSROADS**

PARAPHRASED CONNECTIONS

A simple way to get to know how you might define any situation is to begin describing it in different ways as if you were trying to explain it to various people and groups, i.e., finding **other ways to say the same thing** is often the quickest method for understanding what you really mean.

If you chase after an idea before having a clear picture of where you want to go, you may end up being lost.

The task requires searching for the 'right' words which finally 'click' or 'connect' with another person's experiences. In the process of explaining something in many different ways, you can discover the way you think is best for yourself. It's the same as when trying to learn about something new. Eventual understanding only occurs when we begin to see how a **strange new thing** relates to **what we already know.**

For example, depending on whether you were talking to a child, to a college student, or to a criminal, you'd probably use different and specially chosen words to describe the essential relationship between assertiveness and aggression. Likewise, in the process of describing any of your problem situations or goals in varied ways, you'll undoubtedly get to know better what you feel to be essential about them yourself. The results will be your own "bottom line" definitions.

A creative variation of this definition-seeking method is to search for meaningful connections between the strange, new, not yet digested, or understood situation (all of the facts about a particular problem, project, or goal) and more well-known parts of your life.

PRIORITIES

When you know where you're headed, it's hard to get lost. People who don't get what they want from life are generally those people who either don't know what they want or who have fuzzy definitions for what their needs might be.

The centrally important, but too often neglected, definition stage of a design process provides an opportunity for listing and ranking clear priorities or design

69

criteria. Used as a problem-solving method, such criteria listing and ranking applies to any situation, no matter how simple it may be or how complex it may seem.

A successful, efficiently and creatively managed life requires directing the bulk of one's energies to top priorities and paying attention to everything else in the order of their lesser importances. But, for most people, memorable successes are few. It's far more common to spread one's energy far and wide, jumping from one attraction to another, rather than prorating one's energies according to consciously determined priorities.

The method works this way:
A. Make a random list of everything you can think of that might be important to the successful realization of the situation at hand. Don't worry about what comes first or what might be repeated; just generate possibilities.

B. Review the list and organize it by gathering together those parts which seem closely related or integral. Rewrite the list until you think that its different components are clearly and distinctly identified.

C. Examine each component group individually and comparatively, attempting to determine which one or ones are of first importance, which second, etc.

D. Conclude by deriving a statement of primary focus based on the group with the highest priority rating. After reviewing the statement, if it still feels good, go with it. It's the best you can do at this time.

*Having a situation
clearly defined,
is like having your finger
on its pulse.*

TALK IT OUT; WRITE IT OUT

The direct experience of getting intimate with someone or something is a proven method for finding out what they're really all about. It takes more effort than the normal approach of "merely thinking about it," but it usually produces a great deal more insight in a lot less time.

Talking and writing freely, with more concern for meaning rather than with formal grammar or diction, will get you headed directly toward a basic understanding of the issue(s) at hand. To derive knowledge about something by translating your thoughts and feelings into written or spoken words may seem obvious or superficial at the outset but once you get 'a foot in the door,' deeper meanings can then be developed.

Productive as it is, this simple technique is rarely given the respect it deserves. Perhaps, because people are reluctant to verbalize by falsely assuming that breaking the inertia of silence or the void of a blank page becomes an irreversible commitment or because talking and writing seem too simple to be worthwhile. Either cause is an imaginary negative barrier. The creative importance of verbalization exists in the activity itself, the behavior which identifies someone seeking meaning or testing values in what they're doing.

Variation: hang a sheet of paper containing an open request for viewpoints regarding your situation in a public place. Since few people can resist the urge to add their opinion to a list containing other people's opinions (especially when no pressure or signature is involved), such a list has an inertia of its own.

KEY WORDS

Using felt pen highlighters in text books and lecture notes is the standard college method for identifying key issues. Some books even come pre-edited with the important parts repeated in some special way off to the side. This tag-on variation of the previous method can also be used as a more objective way to "get to the bottom" of an issue by compressing it into key expressions.

After reading or reviewing what you have said, written or read, go back over it with a highlighter to make the important definitive content stand out clearly. Underscoring, circling, starring, use of brackets, wiggly lines, etc. will all do the job nicely.

Then, rewrite the specially identified, highlighted material on a separate sheet, continually trying to abstract its essential meaning still further. For example: the underscored words in the previous text reveal the essential meaning or intended message of the entire text:

"Use of highlighters (is) an objective way to abstract essential meaning."

SYNECTICS

Synectics, the brainchild of educator and author William J.J. Gordon, is an all-purpose method with a potential for generating deep, philosophical definitions. (It is also useful for producing fresh ideas or simply for general practice in creative thought and behavior.) The technique is described in detail in several books by Gordon and his associates following his original publication of *Synectics*, in 1961. Basically, it is a psychology-based method for **developing insight from out-sight**. The title-term, translated from Greek roots, means "the joining together of apparently different and irrelevant objects."

Actually, Synectics is more than a method. It is a near-complete problem-solving process (an **"excursion"**, as Gordon calls it) and includes a variety of methods. Conscious use of Synectics methodology can become an enjoyable creative behavior learning game as well as an exercise for maintaining creative agility.

Try not to suppress any meaning until you're sure that you have determined what you consider to be the "bottom line" or essential meaning.

Synectics theory includes **four BEHAVIORAL paths** to creative problem solving:

1. LEARNING DETACHMENT AND INVOLVEMENT
Developing the ability to stand apart from a subject in order to view it objectively as well as the ability to get into its truths by breaking through the external shell

2. LEARNING TO DEFER JUDGMENT
Developing the ability to objectively consider a subject without judging its acceptability

3. LEARNING TO SPECULATE
Developing the ability to fantasize, pose questions, and make suppositions

4. ALLOWING A SUBJECT TO HAVE LIFE
Thinking of things as autonomous; as having lives of their own; enjoying mutual participation with situations and processes in lieu of solely controlling them.

The "mechanisms" used in Synectics to facilitate learning those four primary creative behaviors are **analogies**, **metaphors**, and **similes**; three language forms which expedite the importance of "looking at one thing and seeing another."

72

Synectics "excursions" utilize a sequence of question-response events using all three forms.

1. DIRECT ANALOGY
Determining how any two things are related to one another; the continuous search for the ultimate relationship between all things; for example: "How is this thing similar to that thing?"

2. PERSONAL ANALOGY
Becoming sympathetic (often to the level of empathy) to various situational conditions in order to become aware of internal problems not clearly seen from the outside; designing scenarios; role-playing. Ex.: "How does it feel to be like and behave like...?"

3. COMPRESSED CONFLICT
Creating a two-word poetic paradox (oxymoron) to express the transference experienced in Step 2. Searching for incongruity ("problems within problems") in order to force a coming to grips with key internal problems; thus deriving deeper understanding of a situation.

For practical purposes, a Synectics excursion can be viewed as having **three general stages**: 1. Analysis, 2. Stretch (detachment), and 3. Fresh View point.

STAGE ONE calls for analyzing the situation by examining **initial viewpoints**, criticizing assumed relationships and preconcepts and restating the problem or goal. **STAGE TWO** requires **detachment** from the problem/goal by examining other apparently dissimilar situations. The keyword here is "stretch"; making sure that the analogy used is clearly 'detached' from the original situation. **STAGE THREE** returns from the 'unrelated' voyage with **fresh experience and viewpoints** which can then be applied to the problem.

In a nutshell, Synectics provides a path to new insight, allowing you to "stretch" your limits of understanding by removing the onus of responsibility for a 'personal' problem...at least temporarily.

NOTE: Because it can easily include many stopping points along the way, a formalized Synectics excursion may require upwards of two hours to complete. However, used separately and/or informally, any of its mechanisms can produce results in mere seconds.

Practice with the Synectics process helps remind us of the basic physical-ecological connection: all things are interrelated; everything is related to everything else; everything is the same thing.

RECIPES AND FORMULAE

If, in fact, 'there's nothing new under the sun' and 'everything's been said or done before,' why hassle yourself by attempting to invent a new definition from scratch? There is undoubtedly a proven formula already in existance which could easily carry you to a successful solution and/or conclusion without having to reinvent it. Go to the library. Get out the reference materials. Dig out a proven path to success and see how it feels in terms of what you're trying to achieve.

Every researcher, philosopher, historian, theologian, teacher, or expert in any subject who ever derived a recipe and wrote it down is fair game as a helpmate in your search for meaning and direction. It's also possible that some of these "proven formulae" might be altered and/or combined to better suit your own particular needs. That's generally how advancements occur.

PROBLEMS WITHIN PROBLEMS

Creative problem-solving researchers have defined the word **"problem"** as being **"a situation in need of improvement"**, another way of saying "something is wrong and needs fixing." Paraphrased into **goal-seeking** terminology, a definition might be restated as "something is wanted and needs getting".

This method suggests that the key to resolving any dilemma lies in isolating that particular part of a situation that's most wrong (needs "fixing" the most). It implies that **finding the principal problem within the problem** and then **fixing it** will, in turn, resolve the entire problem.

Example: a school system not producing satisfactory results might be improved by determining which one of its potential internal problems is the crucial one and, by 'fixing' that area, thereby resolving the overall problem. The crucial problem could relate to any one of many possibilities. If, by analysis, it was decided that "poor student attitude" was really the cause beneath the problem, a new program in motivation and positive thinking for students might be all it takes to bring the entire system back up to snuff.

BOIL IT DOWN (ESSENCE-FINDING)

A fine natural floral perfume is the product of distilling thousands of blossoms to the point of permanently embodying the essential aroma of a single living flower. It requires the boiling-down of many parts of a thing in order to capture its true, underlying scent. Done well, the process takes patience and effort. Seeking the essential meaning or essence of a problem/goal situation is a similar distillation process.

Truly effective essence-finding is built on the information gleaned from a previously completed, comprehensive analysis (Stage Two). When the essentials of that analysis are reviewed and then digested into a more compact form, a definition results. The quality of the eventual "essence" is directly related to the quality and depth of the analysis.

During the initial stage of analytical review, the essence-seeking problem-solver alternates between two tasks: **1. Identifying the relationships** between all major data components, and **2.** Seeking to identify the **relative importances** of those relationships in order to determine the "most essential" one(s).

MISSION OBJECTIVE(S)

Work invested in clarifying objectives is usually well-rewarded. It not only helps remove the confusion from problem-solving, it also lights up the path to success. Objectives are the same as **goals**: specific intentions; things that are wanted. When goals are stated in measurable terms, they serve as established standards for a successful mission. In the end, the degree of success attained is measured by them.

Objectives are best achieved by design, i.e., defined, delineated, and systematically realized. Successful transportation systems and space programs, for example, are completely dependent on **clearly defined objectives**. Achieving what their owners, planners, engineers, pilots and operators expect or intend to achieve is essential to their safe, continual, profitable operation.

75

To successfully translate any 'dream' into clear achievement, i.e., to fulfill any design intention, depends on stating and striving to reach clearly measurable objectives. Sounds easy, doesn't it? Well, it is easy and yet, it isn't. Since objectives are destinations, it would seem that we could simply set the course and, by going in that direction, eventually reach them. But, it's not always that simple, especially when objectives remain abstract or in any way fuzzy. In the end, knowing how well you've succeeded requires knowing how far you wanted to go. The key is **measurement**.

'Fuzzy' destinations can be separated from achievable ones by asking the test question: **"How will I know when I've reached it?"** If the answer is still fuzzy, more clarification is required. At times it may become necessary to pose a continuous series of such questions before something tangible occurs.

A case in point is the common, almost universal abstract desire to achieve happiness. The objective stated in its fuzzy form, "get happy," is rarely realized. Attaining happiness is a highly personal and relative objective and there are many possible directions for reaching it. But, seeking a clear answer to the question "How will I know when I've achieved it?" can provide the stuff needed to stay on course in the direction of your personally defined happiness. Until you can recognize the signs and behaviors of happiness and head in that direction, happiness merely remains an unfulfilled dream; a "sometimes thing," not dependably under your control. You surely wouldn't opt to travel on a supersonic aircraft operating on a similarly unclear basis.

Another common, but often fuzzy goal is **to become well-known and/or to make a lot of money.** That popular dream of **fame and fortune** keeps the vast majority of society confused and running around in circles. As long as public recognition and wealth remain indefinite, it's hard to know where to begin. Clear objectives, however, make it much easier to know where to start and how to proceed. As soon as it becomes clear what is really meant by 'fame' and what the limits of 'fortune' really encompass, the gateway to one or both opens up.

Definitive knowledge points out where the gaps and conflicts exist in personal value systems. As soon as one destination is clarified, it becomes much easier to see further possibilities, to plan new goals, to see bigger and better rainbows and/or personal "pots of gold."

CROSSROADS

Problem-solving and goal-seeking excursions into uncharted, unmarked areas require choosing between paths and directions at every fork and crossroad along the way. Road forks and crossroads are, of course, metaphors for **contradictory information** and **ambivalence.** Taking the wrong road at a fork or becoming distracted and turned 90 degrees off course at a crossroad is a common occurance. Apparent facts pull us in divergent directions and sometimes two or more of our beliefs just don't agree in principle. Such experiences tend to make most travelers nervous. But, for someone aware of the need for definition, an unmarked fork in their path merely serves a creative opportunity rather than a frustrating dilemma.

In short, if your road develops a "fork", use the occasion positively as an opportunity: another situation-defining technique for uncovering previously obscure meanings or unseen directions.

Guidebooks for
Definition

Forget all the rules about graphic design; Gill, Bob; Watson/Guptill; New York; 1985

Synectics; Gordon, William J.J.; The Macmillan Co.; New York; 1970

The Doors of Perception; Huxley, A.; Harper & Row; New York; 1970

The Hidden Dimension; Hall, Edward T.; Doubleday; Garden City, NY; 1966

The Measurement of Meaning; Osgood, C.E.; Suci, G.J.; Tannenbaum, P.H.; University of Illinois Press; Urbana; 1957

On Knowing; Bruner, Jerome; Atheneum Press; New York; 1965

The **Fourth Stage** on a
Systematic Problem-Solving Voyage is
Ideation

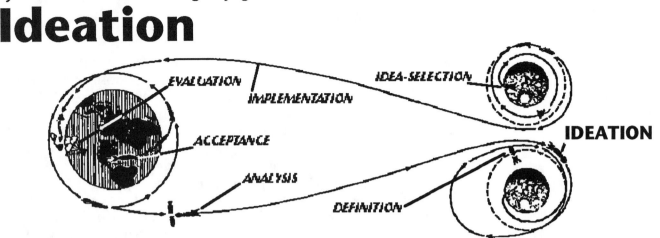

Ideas are **ways**; ways to **go places** and **do things**. They are the **alternatives** or **options** for resolving problems or reaching goals. **Ideation**, a **divergent thinking stage**, is the first sub-stage of Synthesis. Once a problem situation or goal has been defined in clearly solvable (achievable) terms, the search begins for the best **way** to bring it to a successful conclusion.

Because they aren't well understood, ideas are generally thought of as something magical; things that appear "out of the blue" to "save the day"; things that strike, like welcome lightning bolts of inspiration, without warning or help; a blessing. It follows that some people are thought to be more blessed than others. Idea-people, therefore, enjoy a kind of social reverence.

A **creative person** is commonly defined as "**someone with ideas.**" When others are confused and you have 'ready' ideas on the tip of your tongue, people tend to look to you as someone with know-how. The truth is that everyone has the potential for generating ideas, not just a select few. The saying, "**Ideas are a dime a dozen**" is a truism. Ideas aren't hard to find when you know how to find them. And, they're especially easy to find when understood as possible solutions to clearly defined problems or as pathways to known goals.

Normal problem-solving behavior is impulsive; taking action on the first idea that comes along. A more creative approach is to consider many ideas before selecting one as the best way to go. For example, professional photographers know that a proven method for achieving a few good pictures is to take lots of pictures and to then select the best from the lot. Lots of ideas are generally better than just a few ideas. Having a greater menu of choice simply improves the odds for success. When you have five ideas for solving a problem or reaching a goal, instead of just one, you have four additional, possibly better ways to achieve what you're after. Your position is less limited and you provide a greater creative potential for dealing with the situation at hand.

Ideas logically follow definitions in the sense that we don't need a way to get there until we have a place to go. In reverse, having an idea (a way to go) before having a definition (destination) is like having an airline ticket without a travel plan.

But remember, just as it makes sense to consider many ways to get to a destination before deciding that one of them is the best way, it's also possible that, even though you may have developed some sense of self-achievement by getting this far, deriving a unique, inspirational idea at this time might alter your course of events by suggesting changes in previously defined plans.

Try not to worry about changes in your plans. A new idea may be a blessing in disguise. It might allow you to get a better view of what was really needed or wanted all the time.

In any event, since all ideas are merely optional possibilities for reaching destinations, there will probably be a "next time" for any ideas left behind in the decision-making stage which follows.

Most of all, ideation can provide a refreshing lighthearted break in what may well have been very serious business up until now.

Concepts (definitions) are destinations; ideas are ways to get there (options); two distinctly different meanings, although often used interchangeably.

Language Guide
To IDEATE a Problem Situation is..
...to generate various means for reaching a solution
...to find optional ways to realize a definition
...to look at all the cards before making a play!
...to suggest various strategies
...to lay out the spectrum of alternatives
...to create a menu of pathways to a specific goal

Methods for
Ideation

Alternative Ways
for Generating Options
in Problem-Solving or Goal-Seeking

Remember: Ideas are merely possibilities and not yet decisions. They need not be evaluated in terms of how unique or earth-shaking they appear to be. (After all, you'll be throwing most of them out in the next stage anyway as you determine whether or not they are viably related to your objectives.) If you, like most other people, judge the value of your thoughts one by one, you'll probably generate very few options in the long run. But, if you can allow yourself to forego any idea-evaluations and just let your thoughts be heard, you'll soon have a long list of possibilities or options from which to pick and choose the best.

Here is a menu of techniques for generating ideas. If one method doesn't seem to work well for you, try others. In the end, the more techniques you can master, the more versatile you'll become for dealing with the many and varied problem-solving demands of living.

1. BRAINSTORMING: THE BASIC METHOD
2. BRAINSTORMING TEAMS
3. BRAINSTORMING: CRAZY IDEAS
4. SYNECTICS IDEATION:TAKE A BREAK
5. ATTRIBUTE WEAVING
6. FORCED CONNECTIONS
7. OTHER PLACES
8. WHAT IF...?
9. MANIPULATIVE VERBS
10. LATERAL THINKING
11. INVENTION; THE NEW WAY

Good ideas don't come automatically. The more options you have, the more chances you have for one of them being right on target.

BRAINSTORMING;
THE BASIC METHOD

Back in 1953, before the subject of creativity had been much researched, the highly creative Madison Avenue

80

advertising executive, Alex Osborn, wrote a book titled *Applied Imagination.* In it, he outlined a method for quickly generating lots of ideas which he dubbed **Brainstorming**.

Over the years, Osborn's technique has become the definitive basic method for finding ideas. Today, it continues, with several variations, to be just as valuable. In the interim, the term Brainstorming has unfortunately been translated into many forms of usage. The word, as currently used, can mean anything from "just thinking about it" to "very formal systematic ideation." Although the primary value of the method is to produce many ideas quickly, it's not unusual for someone with but a single idea to paradoxically declare "I just had a brainstorm" (only one idea!).

Observing an experienced Brainstorming team at work is a sure way to sell yourself on the power of this proven method. Even first-time, inexperienced groups generally boggle the minds of viewers by producing an average of **ten ideas per minute**. It certainly beats the normal production rate of struggling for an hour or more to think up a mere two to three alternatives. Brainstorming effectiveness depends both on what you want it to do for you and the degree of formality considered appropriate to such use. Whether applied privately, personally and casually or adhering to strict rules in formal groups, the results tend to match the performance.

Most people who say they've tried Brainstorming and found it to be ineffective probably haven't tried it formally, which has **two basic requisites**: First, it's necessary to **ask a proper idea-seeking question**, and secondly, **four rules must be followed. Both** requirements are **crucial** to Brainstorming effectiveness.

An **idea-seeking question** is one which begs for options to a specific problem. The classic example begins with **"What are all the ways...?"** For instance, the question "What are all the ways to save water?" seeks various alternatives to a specific concern for water conservation. The importance of including the word *all* must be emphasized to ensure a nonrestrictive, open-minded approach to the Brainstorming session. Also, the more definitive the question can be, the more relevant will be all responses to it. Without a clearly directed question, results tend to be equally indefinite, distracting and/or confusing.

After an appropriate question has been formulated,

If you don't know where you're headed, you could easily end up someplace else!

81

there are four **Brainstorming principles**, which, in practice, become **'rules'** to follow. Although the four rules are fairly simple to understand, they do require creative behaviors which aren't so common and which tend to contradict typical, normal adult habits.

The Four Rules of Brainstorming

1. Quantity is wanted. The primary purpose for using an ideation method is to generate ideas. Whatever it takes to get you moving should be tried. Sure, it's going to be work, perhaps hard work. But wouldn't you willingly devote about 10 minutes of work to generate 10 to 20 possible solutions to your problem?? O.K. then, if you're really serious about this, get busy and don't stop until you have a long list of ideas.

2. Free-wheeling is necessary. If you are going to allow ideas to start flowing, you'll have to open the gate and let them out. You can't generate quantity if you're restricting free-flowing possibilities in any way. Most people resist this rule out of fear of saying or doing something "silly"; the same reason that people fail to ask questions when they know they need information. Behaving freely is best described by the term **'permissive'**. Remember: Because you allow yourself to think and behave freely for 10 minutes, doesn't mean that you, as a person, have been permanently changed into a weirdo free-wheeler. It does suggest, however, that you can control your behavior when necessary.

3. Defer Judgment. The most restrictive deterrent to the flow of ideas is to behave like a normal adult and consider each individual idea judgmentally as it occurs. In our 'growing up' process, we learn to be decisive about everything as it happens. Now, when we need to defer judgment, that habit get's in our way. The key is to realize that when you are generating options, you are not deciding on ideas. Decision-making comes later; after a large number of alternatives are available. Then, you'll be able to judge all of them equally and fairly. If you judge before you deal yourself a full hand, you're playing like an amateur. Bite your tongue when you find yourself getting critical.

4. Tag-On. When the flow stops, you can always start right up again by making more out of what you already have. So, if you've said it once, say it again...just change it a little. Grab onto a part of a previous idea and give it a twist. Voila! A new idea.

Once you learn how to generate ideas quickly, people will probably start to think of you as a creative sort of person.

The basic **Brainstorming Process** works like this:

Establish a time limit. 10 to 15 minutes should be plenty for a casual pace. If you are really following the rules intensely, you'll be worn out in 5 minutes.

Write out your idea-seeking question using paper, recorder, computer monitor or blackboard,

Review the four behavioral Brainstorming rules and follow them. Focus on the four rules instead of worrying about how incomplete, disorderly or foolish things might look to someone else. Write down just enough of each idea to clearly identify it as a separate alternative or possibility and move to the next idea.

Afterwards, rewrite your 'mess' into a neater, more legible and complete list. Redo it again, if necessary.

That's all it takes to make Brainstorming an effective and efficient part of your thinking tool-kit. With it, you can have a list of alternatives, options, or ideas in 5 to 10 minutes anytime you desire.

BRAINSTORMING TEAMS

The professional approach to Brainstorming has always been to utilize a knowledgeable group or team of participants. Team members not only provide good additions for idea tagging-on, they also serve as mutual watchdogs for obeying the four 'official rules' and staying in line with the defined problem or goal.

Team preparation includes group research, conference and participation in formulating and discussing idea-seeking questions and a review of Brainstorming rules. Follow-up 'debriefing' sessions held at a later date also allow for additional post-session ideas to be aired and added to the list originally generated.

BRAINSTORMING: CRAZY IDEAS

Beginners at creative problem-solving cringe when confronted by an 'off-the-wall' idea in a Brainstorming session. Consequently, all 'questionable' ideas are generally held back or repressed because they seem troublesome to explain, worthless, or even worse, "**crazy**." But, if you're looking for **uniqueness** or if in any way you'd like your ideas to be **provocative**, it's highly probable that those same normally discarded "crazy ideas" offer the most creative potential.

This method is a Brainstorming variation which makes it a point to '**care for the crazies**.' It requires being on the lookout for ideas which seem to be offbeat for one reason or another. After a regular Brainstorming session, scan your list of ideas for the ones that brought a smile to your face when they were proposed. (Note: Smiles and other facial 'distortions' are clues that something unusual is afoot.) Form new idea-seeking questions based on the crazy ideas and Brainstorm them again. Once more, extract the crazies from those sessions and repeat the process until you are satisfied that your results are positive.

Example: In a team Brainstorming session built around the question "What are all the ways to learn a second language?" everyone smiled when one member proposed "become reborn to foreign parents" because 'it seemed so impossible.' Noticing the reaction, the leader tagged the idea for a follow-up session based on the new question "What are all the ways to become reborn to foreign parents?" where responses didn't appear to be silly at all. Some were actually more creative than ideas judged as "acceptable" in the first session. Because it was saved instead of being discarded, the 'silly' idea opened up several new lines of thinking about the original problem. Some second session responses were also somewhat 'crazy,' thus inviting other sessions, etc.:

"adopt a foreign family by mail"
"visit them during vacation" (tag-on)
"become a parent by caring for a foreign child"
"adopt a foreign child" (tag-on)
"buy and read foreign children's books"
"eat meals in foreign family restaurants"
"become 'born again' in a foreign church group"
"invite foreigners into your church" (tag-on)

Try not to hold back any idea no matter how goofy it might seem at the time. Let all the ideas flow. The secret to finding a few good ideas is to screen them from lots of ideas... afterwards!

4 SYNECTICS IDEATION: TAKE A BREAK

Synectics (See P. 72) is a process wherein "the joining together of apparently different and irrelevant objects"

84

is a means for formulating fresh viewpoints (definitions) and related ideas.

In the final phase of a Synectics session, the problem-solver returns to the originally stated problem refreshed from successfully dealing with extraneous issues. New ways (ideas) of dealing with fresh viewpoints abound in such a unique environment. Similar psychology can work to enhance ideation at other times, too. The method: **TAKE A BREAK!** Get away from your situation by getting into something else for a while.

Read about something else. Go to the movies. Talk to different people about different things. Ride from one end of a bus or subway route to the other and return still another way. Then, if you've been interested enough in the other, supposed "unrelated" experiences and got to know something new about them, when you return to your own situation, you'll probably have a new 'slant' on those old problems and perhaps some new ideas as well.

ATTRIBUTE WEAVING

Inertia is both a help and a hindrance. It keeps things at rest and hard to start and yet, once started, it helps make it easy to keep going. Once things get moving, one step leads to another. Here's a method that may help you deal with the inertia of 'wondering and waiting to discover what to do next' by allowing you to dream up lots of inventive ideas.

First, review your defined problem or goal situation to **determine** its **general attributes**. What are the key ingredients? Traits? Characteristics? Issues? List those qualities as column headings on paper or blackboard. Example: A goal defined as "I must find a way to pay off my auto loan four months early (by June) in order to be able to go to Brazil in September" might be said to have the following key attributes (among others): "monthly car loan payments"; "salary"; "other expenses"; "Brazil"; "travel costs"; etc.

Second, under each column heading, try to **list the sub-attributes** of the key ingredients by considering them from as wide a range of points of view as possible; including their appropriate physical, functional, psychological, social, or economical characteristics.

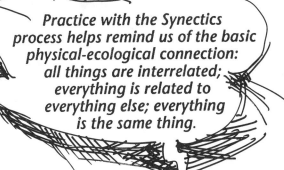

Practice with the Synectics process helps remind us of the basic physical-ecological connection: all things are interrelated; everything is related to everything else; everything is the same thing.

85

Continuing with the example of the 'car loan-travel plan' situation, some attributes listed under the heading "other expenses" might be: Rent, Food, Parking, Dining out for lunch, Laundry, New suit and shoes, Entertaining friends, Video rentals, etc.

Third, when the lists start to develop, and forward inertia is active, start **fooling around** with the facts by interweaving various bits and pieces of your lists into new "fabrics of ideas." Example: If you interweave the various expenses of 'food', 'lunching out,' and 'entertaining friends,' you might quickly imagine saving a bundle of money (for the car payment) by "entertaining a friend at lunch on food you economically prepared and brought from home." Many other ideas for solving the problem situation by way of economy without hardship are hidden with your lists. The possibilities are endless. All you have to do is "weave" what you already know into some possibilities not previously evident. Having fun helps.

FORCED CONNECTIONS

An interesting variation of the previous method derives from an analogy found in the literature of creative behavior. It relates the **human brain** to the child's toy called a **kaleidoscope** by suggesting that the brain, which contains a varied assortment of data (bits and pieces of experience), is like a kaleidoscope which contains various glass and plastic fragments. And that, similar to the way a kaleidoscope can be rotated to achieve uniquely different patterns, so can the data contained in a brain be manipulated to produce an assortment of new relationships.

The analogy further suggests that, although a brain might be restricted from receiving any new data, as might occur if a person were in solitary confinement for a lengthy period, that ever-new ideas could still be constructed from all previously held data by simply 'rotating' those old bits and pieces into new patterns.

Translated into an idea-finding method, you should be able to generate enumerable ideas by simply forcing new interconnections between the bits and pieces of data you have already collected in your voyage through the analysis and definition phases of the problem-solving process.

OTHER PLACES

Lateral Thinking and Synectics methods both suggest getting away from the problem as a means of gaining insight by way of 'out-sight'. Such external overviews are also practical ways to spot ideas.

From outside of the problem, it's easier to see possibilities for realizing planned improvements. Many of the alternative avenues, previously blocked from view by being too close, can be examined that way. So, if you've been working on generating ideas and still feel that something's missing, get outside of it for a while by getting into some other situations or environments. When you return, you'll probably uncover new ideas based on your sidetrip experiences.

WHAT IF...?

There are two kinds of experience: real and imagined. Ideally, each supports the other, but at times, it's hard to separate the two. What is real and what's imagined can get very intertwined. So-called 'real' experiences are different for everyone. Because our individually perceived viewpoints are combinations of what we are sensing and what we already know, there are as many versions of reality as there are people to perceive them. Being alert to which parts of 'reality' might be merely imaginary can save lots of unnecessary problems. Developing a "controlled imagination" is a good way to have ideas whenever you need them.

Controlled imagination is a form of managed free-wheeling; similar to one of the rules of Brainstorming. It is different from random daydreaming in the sense that when imagination runs freely, outside of your control, the 'experiences' produced either relate to what you're doing or not. Relevance becomes a matter of chance. When you control your fantasies, you make relevant images happen, i.e., you improve the odds for having meaningful daydreams.

Actually, either form of free-wheeling imaginative adventure is positive when searching for ideas. Both daydreams and controlled images are free from restrictive ties to reality and therefore useful techniques for fantasizing and cost-free experimentation.

Suppose, for example, you are faced with the problem of upgrading your home office and need ideas for selling your old computer. **Here's how a managed imagination might work:** Close your mind to other reality close at hand by foccussing on your fantasy. You might begin by imagining the old machine to be out of work, on the street, homeless..a piece of discarded "hardluck hardware"...but still highly skilled and able to take on all sorts of creative tasks. Continue your day-dreaming by imagining that the computer can actually think and speak for itself and that it decides to advertise for a new owner. (**STOP!** Note that each ad you might write in the computer's name is going to be a possible idea for actually selling it.) Going further, you next imagine that the machine gets responses to its ads. (**STOP!** Note that each response presents questions from possible buyers... more ideas for you). Etc. Etc.

MANIPULATIVE VERBS

Manipulative Verbs, another Alex Osborn technique from his book *Applied Imagination*, will also trigger other free-wheeling idea-generators.

As an advertising executive, Osborn noticed that verbs were used to translate the action of thinking into the words of speech and writing. And, since ideas represent alternative possibilities for taking action, playing around with verbs is like playing around with possible actions. In the process of "manipulating" verbs, new actions (ideas) can be found. Osborn provided a list of nine verbs which he considered to have the most "manipulative" potential. They are: **MAGNIFY, MINIFY, REARRANGE, ALTER, ADAPT, MODIFY, SUBSTITUTE, REVERSE, and COMBINE**. Each one suggests performing some specific operation on any given subject which will "change" it into some alternative form. Voila! Ideas.

Example: Searching for inexpensive, unusual costume and theme ideas for an upcoming DooDah Parade...

88

MAGNIFY: Inflated bags under street clothes
MINIFY: Oversize clothing to make yourself seem tiny or undersize clothing for its humor
REARRANGE: Wear a shirt for pants; pants for a shirt
ALTER: Pants too short; shirt sleeves too long
ADAPT: Last year's costumes with minor changes
MODIFY: Sew pants legs on shirt sleeves
SUBSTITUTE: Office clothes made from trash bags
REVERSE: Wear clothing backwards or upside down
COMBINE: Suit-Dresses for both sexes

Additional verbs which might also produce unique viewpoints are: **ADD, SUBTRACT MULTIPLY, DIVIDE, ELIMINATE, SUBDUE, INVERT, SEPARATE, TRANSPOSE, UNIFY, DISSECT, DISTORT, ROTATE, FLATTEN, SQUEEZE, COMPLEMENT, SUBMERGE, FREEZE, SOFTEN, FLUFF-UP, BY-PASS, LIGHTEN, REPEAT, THICKEN, STRETCH, EXTRUDE, REPEL, PROTECT, SEGREGATE, INTEGRATE, SYMBOLIZE, ABSTRACT, LIGHT-UP,** etc. Your dictionary includes many more.

LATERAL THINKING

Edward DeBono, the British physician better known for his books on creativity, gives us this excellent general-purpose technique for viewing life as a menu containing many possibilities. Not only useful for situational analysis, **Lateral Thinking** is also a simple method for discovering alternative options (ideas). If you find yourself "digging the same hole deeper," branch out by relating what you're doing to some of the many other aspects of life.

INVENTION; THE NEW WAY

If unique is what you seek, go no further. Any of the methods listed in this section can get you there. **Inventiveness is a state of mind,** a willingness to accept an abrupt change from what is normally expected. If the 'inventive' ideas you seek must eventually become socially accepted, use caution. Normal society thrives on the *status quo* and, by definition, is not prone to accepting the abrupt changes related to inventiveness or inventions. People must be "slowly transitioned"; "educated"; "prepared"; "sold".

Inventiveness is easy. All you need do is oppose, change, or complement what everyone normally expects. For example: The normal, expected response to the query "what can we have for supper?" is standard food fare, i.e., something from the menu of normal supper experience. An inventive response would at least change something normal into something abnormal. Answers might include "let's take a walk instead of eating," "let's eat out," "let's try something we haven't eaten before," etc.

The old adage "ideas are a dime a dozen" is true...once you know how to generate them quickly. It's just that most people aren't onto idea-generating methodology. They're normally happy to have a single option to act on. The creative problem-solver knows, as previously said, "having lots of ideas improves the odds for having one good idea."

Making inventive ideas practical, feasible, functional and acceptable is another matter. That takes a bit longer. Most suggestions for abrupt changes in on-going plans require diplomacy and sales acumen. The world is full of die-hards which have to be "sold" everything you propose to accomplish for them. This makes knowledge of human perception and behavior an important component in developing communication skill.

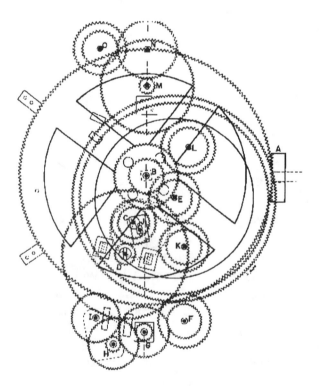

Guidebooks for
Ideation

A Sourcebook for Creative Thinking; Parnes, S. J. and Harding, H.F.; Scribners; New York; 1962

Applied Imagination, Alex F. Osborn, Scribner's, New York, 1963

Brainstorming; Clark, Charles H.; Doubleday; New York; 1958

Conceptual Blockbusting; A Guide to Better Ideas (Second Edition); Adams, James L.; W.W. Norton; New York; 1979

Lateral Thinking; DeBono, Edward; Harper & Row; New York; 1970

Synectics; Gordon, William J.J.; Collier Books; New York; 1961

The Book of Graphic Problem-Solving; Newcomb, John; R.R. Bowker Co.; New York; 1984

Idea-Selection

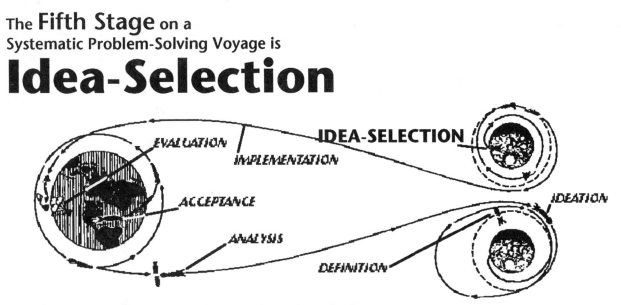

After all ideas are reviewed, sorted and ranked in terms of how well they might help us reach our destinations successfully, it's time to select the best from the batch. **Idea-Selection**, the second sub-stage of Synthesis, is another **convergent thinking** stage. It requires more decision-making.

Selecting involves making comparisons; **matching what you can have with what you want**. If either part is fuzzy, the going will be difficult. How do you know if an idea is a good idea? You check to see how well it might satisfy the previously defined objectives.

Typical problem-solvers, with a less-than-definite understanding of intentions or goals and with few or no ideas from which to choose, approach decision-making with anxiety. They feel helpless. Not only are they fuzzy about what they really want; most of what they could choose from is hidden from them. It's almost like wearing a blindfold when deciding which television to buy, which movie to see, which entree to select from a menu, etc. Added to such uncertainty, decision-making often requires speed, assertiveness, conviction, and the maturity of selecting one or more from a group of many while leaving the rest behind.

An interesting by-product of choosing between options is that the need to become evaluative often causes originally defined plans to change. Although it would seem to be a simple matter to decide which idea or pathway appears "most likely" to take and head that way, it's not always so easy. At times, all options appear to meet our criteria equally and therefore all seem equally "good." Also, it often happens obviously highest ranked or "best idea" isn't our favorite idea for one or more reasons. In either case, the need to review and perhaps revise our previous goals is suggested.

Moreover, once you know how to generate them, ideas never stop coming. While busy evaluating one set of ideas, other, even better, possibilities tend to emerge. Although the combination of alternating back and forth between intentions and ideas and the urge to question previously settled issues from earlier stages can be frustrating, **don't despair!** You won't be confused if you remind yourself of the differences between ideas (ways) and definitions (clear objectives) and how they both interrelate in the problem-solving process. With that awareness, you can easily maneuver amid complications and freely adapt to the changing needs of any particular complex situation.

Decision-making is like deriving definitions. It relates to knowing what you want and to the clarification of values. Understanding the evaluation process and developing your abilities to make decisions are therefore, excellent ways to discover more about yourself and what you believe to be important and, in general, how to get more of what you want out of life.

Language Guide
To SELECT IDEAS
for a Problem Situation is...

...to judge or evaluate relevant alternatives
...to match possibilities with expectations
...to compare what you want with what you
     might be able to have
...to determine the most likely path to success
...to narrow down the field
...to evaluate options
...to choose the best plan of attack for solving a
     problem or reaching a goal
...to screen or filter out the best-fit ideas

Methods for
Idea-Selection

Alternative Ways
for Choosing Between Options
in Problem-Solving or Goal-Seeking

Decision-making is like arriving at a fork in the road; a time for pausing to reflect on which way is the best way to get where you want to go. Again, if the destination is fuzzy and/or the alternative paths aren't relevant, it's a frustrating experience. When you don't know where you're headed, choosing between two alternative paths is every bit as troublesome as having to deal with many different options.

Because being aware of the methods we use is still somewhat rare (a creative behavior), the two most commonly used (normal) techniques for deciding on even the most important of issues are "trial and error" and "guessing" (another way of saying "taking a best shot," "gambling," "going for broke," etc.) Creative "navigators", on the other hand, cooly determine what's best for them by **comparing what they want** (goals or intended resolutions) **with what they can have** (alternative ideas and options). That simple paradigm allows them to stay 'on course' in all sorts of problem situations. And, it doesn't rule out creative experimentation or taking chances (adventure). It merely improves the odds for success.

Comparing options and objectives includes but a small range of methods and variations. Some decision-making methods are long-winded and finicky; others are quicker and not so rigorous. Still, any one of them is better than the common techniques of 'hoping for the best' or 'flipping a coin.'

Some Idea-Selection methods are:
1. WHY NOT TRY 'EM ALL?
2. OPTIONS VERSUS OBJECTIVES
3. TAKE A POLL
4. RANKING AND WEIGHING
5. WHAT COULD HAPPEN IF...?
6. IDEA POTPOURRI
7. DECISION-MAKERS' CHECKLIST

WHY NOT TRY 'EM ALL?

This technique is based on the assumption that problems repeat themselves and that it's not improbable for a problem or goal situation similar to yours to reappear in the future. So, if it seems that "totally solving the problem" is not so crucially imperative at the moment and/or that several of your ideas are obviously worth more consideration before being dumped, why not save them all and simply try each of them one by one over time?

Scientific experimentation shows that the Trial and Error method can be greatly improved by keeping clear, consistent, comparative records. In decision-making terms, each of your ideas can be tested against the same defined criteria, one by one, until the best idea finally emerges as the winner. It's slow and sometimes tedious, but every idea will eventually get a fair shake.

OPINIONS VERSUS OBJECTIVES

Imagine what a fiasco it would be to try judging competitors fairly in a sports event or beauty competition without a checklist of clear criteria. The same is true for any form of fair and reasonable judgement.

Comparing alternative possibilities with intended results is the generic, all-purpose decision-making method. If more of the important decisions in life were resolved this way, there'd be far less need to cope with arbitrary, confusing, and unfair occurances. When you stop to think about it, you'll probably find that it's a rare occasion when you consciously consider either your "criteria" or your "alternatives" prior to making a choice. The word "Oops!" wouldn't be such a common part of our vocabulary if decision-making was a more conscious activity.

The basic version of this method is an X-Y grid connecting all the criteria with all the options. Inside the cells, some consistent form of rating system, such as Yes-No or Plus-Minus, is used to record separate decisions regarding each option relative to each criterion.

At the end of each option column, a tally of the responses in each cell reveals which alternative option(s) gets the most points (wins). Ties must be considered as equals or determined by tie-breakers in the form of additional criteria.

[Note: Teachers face a similar judging situation when grading (evaluating) their students' performance. They know that learning is best achieved when everyone involved knows where they're going and what's expected of them. Where the objectives of a course of study are well prepared, clearly stated and measurable, and presented at the outset of the course, everyone is able to begin working toward the same set of goals. An unstated, unclear, or hidden agenda, keeps students "in the fog" regarding their progress throughout the course. The result is that, at the end, teacher evaluation of student work often lacks consistency and/or objectivity.

Creative students learn quickly that one of the most important keys to academic success is making certain that curriculum and course objectives are clearly defined. Much of their observed "efficiency" comes from knowing what they're supposed to be achieving, instead of worrying or wasting time trying to decipher an uncharted course. When students know what is expected of them, teachers also tend to stay "on course."]

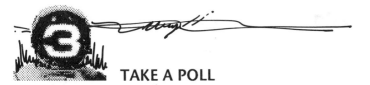

TAKE A POLL

Everyone likes to offer opinions when it appears the outcome won't affect them. And, almost anyone will respond to a questionnaire if it looks easy to fill in, offers some incentive or when there seem to be no "strings attached."

If, in previous stages, you found that getting ideas from others worked well, you might continue to profit from outside help when making decisions regarding which path to follow. Although popular expressions like "I'd rather do it myself," "Let George do it," "I've got to bite the bullet," etc. have somewhat denigrated the potential benefits of asking for someone else's experience, letting others take at least some of "the heat" is still a creative way to deal with decisions.

If you'd like to have your decision gain social acceptability and have the results considered more creative than if you had merely "passed the buck," taking a poll is a simple way to make a decision. You might simply distribute copies of your objectives vs. options comparison chart and let others fill in the ratings which you can tally and average for a collective score.

RANKING AND WEIGHING

You can get more accurate and detailed results when all of your ideas and criteria are comparatively valued in terms of relative rank and weight. Such ranking and weighing of criteria and options on a comparative basis does require some additional calculation. Yet, it's a simple task and often well worth the effort.

For example, when trying to decide which available investment possibility will yield the <u>most profit in the least time</u>, it becomes important to know the order of importance of objectives. In this case, because of the stress on the words "in the least time," the "short-term" criterion would probably be more important than another typical objective such as "Easy payments" yet, perhaps less important than "No cash down payment." It is clear that all three criteria have different levels of value. The degree of their separate values becomes a factor in the final decision.

The simplest technique for determining the ranked order of any number of ideas or criteria is a **matrix** or chart containing two identical lists of the items to be ranked in a horizontal-vertical relationship. Since each item intersects with every other item within the matrix, the connecting cells become points of decision.

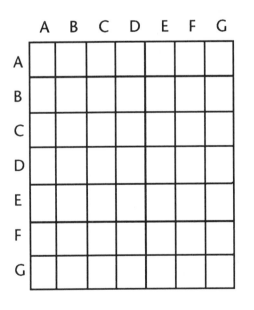

A more efficient version of such a ranking chart is the triangle-shaped **pyramid matrix**. Within the triangle, each entry is compared with all others in terms of one consistently-applied test question: "which of the two is more important?" Variations of the method include additional 'hair-splitting' by including refinements, such as 1 through10 scales, use of 'maybe', etc. After all comparisons are complete, the resulting tally of cells yields a ranked list of entries. Numeric differences between criteria also makes it possible to weigh or "factor" their relative importance or value.

Example: In deciding which one of five houses to rent, you'd probably want to know the ranked order and relative importance of each of various criteria before using them to select from rental possibilities:

In the pyramid, each criterion is identified by a letter and all criteria have interconnecting 'cells'. Which of the two letters eventually goes into those connecting cells is determined by your response to the consistent test question: "which of the two is more important?"

More accurate results are produced if you determine the relative weights of importance by asking "how **much** more important is it?" Twice as important? (2X), Half again as important? (1.5X), Five times more important? (5X). Etc.

For instance, when comparing A. with G., you might decide that <u>being close to your work</u> is twice as important as <u>having a cat</u>. In the cell which connects the two, you would then enter A(2X). An alternative version is waiting until all criteria are ranked and listed before applying their separate relative weights.

Repeating the test question so often and making so ·many related decisions puts you closer in touch with your true feelings about the situation. Perhaps other previously unseen criteria or the need for more options will also become evident in the process. (Note: A Pyramid Matrix contains X times X-1 divided by 2 cells.)

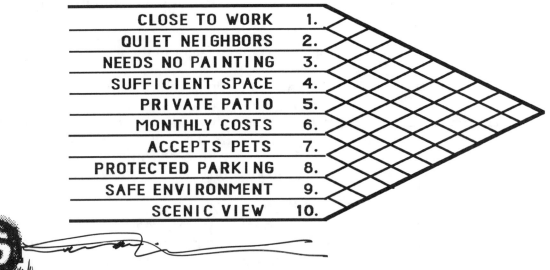

CLOSE TO WORK	1.
QUIET NEIGHBORS	2.
NEEDS NO PAINTING	3.
SUFFICIENT SPACE	4.
PRIVATE PATIO	5.
MONTHLY COSTS	6.
ACCEPTS PETS	7.
PROTECTED PARKING	8.
SAFE ENVIRONMENT	9.
SCENIC VIEW	10.

WHAT COULD HAPPEN IF...?

Because fearing the "worst" is more common than expecting the "best", most people immediately begin **worrying** when faced with decisions. Worry is a distraction; it achieves nothing and is alien to creative behavior.

A more creative, not-so-commonly-used method replaces worry with positive thinking and imagination. With this technique, both the **"best and worst situation"** scenarios about each alternative are generated.

After experiencing (via imagination) the best, as well as the worst results, reasons for decisions (criteria) become clear and selecting the best is less confusing.

Using the following example, **try it yourself**: Suppose you were faced with having to choose between three "great" business options: **1.** a high-paying, fast-paced corporate job in Chicago, **2.** a lesser-salaried but more relaxed job managing a seaside resort in Hawaii, or **3.** a median-salaried, self-managed position traveling world-wide, expenses paid, as a company diplomat.

Taking each of the three options, one by one, go twice through the high points of an imaginary "day on the job"; first, enjoying only the "benefits"; second, suffering all of the problems. After your six mini-excursions, you'll surely have a better understanding of the options. Your criteria will certainly be improved by having been put to the test at every turn. Resulting final decisions will be based on what will be hard to distinguish from 'first-hand' experience.

IDEA POTPOURRI

When seeking to select that **one** idea which best suits your defined criteria, it often happens that no single idea stands out as a winner. Several ideas may seem to have **almost what it takes**, but no one of them has **all** that's necessary. What then?

No matter how unacceptable a group of ideas might seem to be, every idea has at least some possibility of viability; some small bit of merit, if, for no other reason than it was originally proposed as a possible solution to the situation at hand.

The gist of the **potpourri method** is to take the **best parts of several ideas** and rework them to form a new **composite idea**. Example: Suppose that when seeking to 'improve your <u>attitude</u> toward your job,' you defined the problem as 'improving your work <u>environment</u>.' You now have half a dozen ideas and you are still indecisive; no single idea seems to really "grab" you. They are: Re-arrange the furniture; get new furniture; get more sunlight; make the place more "special"; paint up-fix up; change colors, etc.

Using the potpourri technique, you could avoid being dissatisfied with any single idea by combining some small bit of each of your alternative possibilities into something perhaps more acceptable...moving things around, adding a few fresh, bright colors, buying one new piece of furniture, opening the shades to let in some sunlight, etc. The overall result will probably meet your defined expectations more satifactorily.

7 DECISION-MAKERS' CHECKLIST

Three primary factors are included in all decisions: Criteria or Definition (what you want or expect in a good solution), **Options** or ideas (what you can have; alternative ways of reaching goals and expectations) and the **Relationship** between the two (criteria versus options). Each of the three factors can be further sub-divided into finer parts or particulars.

The following method provides a checklist of possible decision-making pitfalls might help you locate and manage any snags you might encounter on your journey. If you are having trouble making a decision of any kind, within any situation, no matter how seriously important or trivial the outcome might be, you can depend on finding the problem in one of these areas.

A. Criteria too general. Directions, goals or expectations are not sufficiently clear or specific. You need to be more "definitive" about what you expect!

B. Criteria ambivalent. Expectations contain internal confusions and/or conflicts. Before deciding on other things, you must first come to grips with how you intend to "have your cake and eat it too."

C. Criteria insufficient. Too open-ended; not enough to go on. What other things are important?

D. Criteria overbearing. Too much is wanted at one time. You might have to decrease the number of your demands and save the rest for another time.

E. Options too similar. All your ideas are the same idea. No real choice is available. You need to add other, different possibilities to your list of ideas.

F. Options too few. Not enough alternatives are available to make choosing seem worthwhile. Probably, you need to spend more time with ideation.

G. Options too many. Alternatives are lost in the crowd. You need to sort and classify your options and arrange them in groups so that they might be dealt with more fairly.

H. Criteria and Options unrelated. Ideas aren't offering clear paths toward achieving objectives. Connections between what is wanted and possible ways to get it aren't clear. You might be on the "wrong track"!

I. Criteria and Options too similar. Demands are treated like possibilities; ideas are considered as requirements. Keep it straight; you may be forcing the issue.

Remember: It often takes **creative maturity** (courage) to decide in favor of one option and thereby agree to leave the others behind. If you're having a problem making decisions, it may be nothing more than your normal reluctance to take a stand.

Guidebooks for
Idea-Selection

A Method for Measuring Decision Assumptions; Jarrod W. Wilcox, MIT Press, Cambridge, MA, 1972

Decisions (Group Problem-Solving); Hall, Jay; University Books; New York; 1969

Techniques of Evaluation; Sanoff, Henry; University of North Carolina; Raleigh; 1970

The Open and Closed Mind; Rokeach, Milton; Basic Books; New York; 1960

The Science of Decision-Making; Kaufmann, A.; McGraw-Hill; New York; 1968

Your Mind Over Matter; Pilkington, J. Maya and The Diagram Group; Ballantine; New York; 1990

Implementation

Implementation (of a selected idea) is the final stage of Synthesis. To implement is to **fulfill the expectations** (previously **defined**) by translating the best idea(s) into the reality of form and action.

In this near-final step of the overall creative problem-solving process, **convergent and divergent thinking** meet. It's a time where "paying close attention to the road" alternates freely with "taking note of the passing scenery." Theoretically, from here on, reaching a successful conclusion should be easy. If you've been systematic up to this stage, you should have formed a clear picture of your destination, i.e. you should know where you're headed and what you expect to achieve when you arrive. Plus, you should have determined (in the previous stage) the most likely way(s) to get there. If not, you may have to cycle backward to get your situation more clearly organized.

Having passed the pre-flight checkpoints of Acceptance, Analysis, Definition, Ideation, and Idea-Selection, **flight-time has finally arrived**. Implementation means "going for it." All that's left to do is climb aboard and take off.

Implementation becomes the final test of all your planning. It's the moment of truth you've been working toward. But reality is often stranger than fiction. Making something happen invariably opens new areas of possibilities and potential problems. Even though you think you're almost home and that you have everything under control, it's highly likely that additional, unexpected problem-solving "adventures" await you in these final stages of your trip.

The seemingly endless sequence of problems experienced in the life process ceases to be frustrating when we realize that diligence, intelligence, creativity and process awareness help make problems manageable and goals attainable. They do cost us energy. They provide no assurance of success. Occasionally, they cause us to fail. Still, they're the best we have.

Implementation means action (a verb form). Although all verbs describe some form of action, the following specific verb gerunds may help reinforce the fact that it takes action to "make dreams come true":

ACTING... ACCEPTING... AGREEING... ALLOWING... ALTERING... ANNOUNCING... ADAPTING... ANALYZING... AIDING... ADMINISTERING... BAKING... BANKING... BALANCING... BARTERING... BOMBING... BIKING... BLOCKING... BRAINSTORMING... BREAKING... BUDGETING... BUILDING... BUYING... CARING... CLEANING... COMPOSING... COOKING... DANCING... DESIGNING... DETAILING... DIGGING... DIVIDING... DRAWING... DRIVING... EASING... EATING... ENJOYING... FACILITATING... FINDING... FLYING... GRASPING... GREETING... HELPING... INVENTING... INVESTING... ITEMIZING... JESTING... JOINING... JUMPING... KISSING... LEARNING... LECTURING... LISTING... MAILING... MANAGING... MASSAGING... MENDING... MEMORIZING... MOURNING... MINING... MIXING... MOBILIZING... MULTIPLYING... NAMING... NESTING... NEUTRALIZING... NIBBLING... OWNING... PAINTING... PAYING... PEACE-MAKING... PLANNING... PLAYING... QUENCHING... RANKING... RATING... RECORDING... REMODELING... REVISING... REPORTING... RESEARCHING... RUNNING... READING... SAILING... SECURING... SCULPTING... SEEING... SELLING... SENDING... SOOTHING... SPENDING... TEACHING... TELLING... TERMINATING... TESTING... TRAVELING... VALUING... WINING & DINING... WRITING... X-RAYING... ZEROING-IN, ETC.

Don't forget to carry along some spare ideas just in case the one you selected as 'best' fails to satisfy possibly altered expectations.

Language Guide
IMPLEMENTION means...
...to act on a decision
...to purposely realize a possibility
...to give physical form to an idea
...to follow a chosen path to success
...to put a plan of action into motion
...to turn fantasy into reality
...to proceed from abstract to concrete
...to **GO FOR IT!**

Methods for
Implementation

Alternative Ways
for Turning Ideas into Realities
in Problem-Solving or Goal-Seeking

Voyages into strange, uncharted territory can become tedious and/or scary. Once again, our natural tendency to take it easy and avoid taking risks often results in our becoming overly lazy or cautious- negative behaviors which must be 'creatively overcome.' Remembering that "it's time to get up and go" or being told to "just do it" are rarely sufficient motivators. We may still need to review our reasons for accepting the problems that were established back in Stage One in order to successfully reach the end.

Having selected a promising idea provides the direction; getting there is something else. Ideas tend to be mere outlines of possible ways to solve problems or move toward goals. Only rarely do even the best of ideas come with detailed operating instructions. There's a big difference between knowing that you want to "fly to New York by way of New Orleans", and knowing what it takes to pull it off without a snag, such as finding the best airline to use; how to get the best-priced tickets; when it's the best time to go; etc. After having an idea, there are still lots of sub-issues to be resolved; lots of minor problems within the general or overall scheme.

One or more of the following techniques may be what you need to reach a successful conclusion.

1. MOMENT OF TRUTH (Brainwashing)
2. TIME AND TASK
3. THE ADVOCATE
4. LIVE UP TO ITS NAME!
5. PERFORMANCE SPECIFICATION
6. EIGHT or more POPULAR ACTION METHODS

Climbing the tree isn't enough. If you want to fly, you'll have to let go of the trunk and 'go out on a limb'!

Creative problem-solving is truly "a process of making dreams come true!" By way of that process, our fantasies, desires, and vague intentions develop, step by step, from abstract dreams into concrete realities.

MOMENT OF TRUTH

By the time you systematically reach the implementation stage, you should have made a commitment to a specific conceptual approach for bringing it into realization. The final task of translating those abstract thoughts and words into something more concrete requires action. It's finally time to make those decisions operational. If your 'defined' problem or goal statement is still fuzzy and not yet stated in measurable terms, any attempt to implement it will become a 'moment of truth.' Some personal 'brainwashing' may be the best technique for finally verbalizing and clarifying the dreams you expect to come true.

TIME AND TASK

"I never seem to have enough time (to do what I really want to do)" is a commonly voiced complaint. But, time is a universal form of energy. Everyone has the same 24-hour resource to be budgeted and managed according to their needs and priorities (intentions). Of course, the creative approach is to "make the necessary time available" for what is wanted in life.

Systematic versions of **time management**, which can range from detailed moment-to-moment operational plans to mere reminders scribbled on a calendar, take many intermediate forms. The generic, model of a **time/task schedule** works like this:

A. List every task that you imagine will need to be performed before your selected plan can be successfully realized. Try answering the question: "what are all the steps that must be taken to make this idea work?" Don't forget to include those **obvious** jobs, like finding supplies and financial backing, etc., which can take the most time and energy to accomplish.

B. Determine the intended time frame or limits, i.e., when you'd like to begin and when you plan to have resolved your problem or reached your goal. Make sure that your intentions are reasonable and that the dates you specify are feasible within your other current general commitments.

C. Make a calendar (time chart) of the time period between beginning and completing your project. Use as much detail as you think the situation warrants. For some, an hourly schedule might be appropriate; for others, perhaps daily, weekly, or monthly goals will be sufficient.

D. Using a progressive sequence, relate your tasks into your time chart sub-divisions. Check to see that you allow enough leeway to account for the unexpected but inevitable "contingencies."

E. Follow your time/task schedule. When a specific task is not completed within its assigned time, it must either be bypassed or added to later time slots. Watch out for doubling-up too much. If the load gets too heavy, you'll be faced with deciding between giving up, starting over, revising your plans, or learning to improve your time management skills.

THE ADVOCATE

You can help your chosen idea become a concrete reality by both getting out in front of it to **pull** and by getting behind it to **push**. The technique of being a supporter or "booster" for what you want to occur is called **advocacy**.

Advocacy, or a lack of it, relates back to the degree of acceptance in the initial process stage. Having zeal for what we do is a proven way of pumping energy into activity. It provides that "extra" life or creative boost that seems to be missing in otherwise 'normal' behavior. As any old-timer jazzman will tell you, "Get hot or go home!" The key behavior here is **enthusiasm**; an active, zealous ambition for success.

LIVE UP TO ITS NAME!

Most people "live up to" their names, nicknames, and titles. They tend to speak, dress, live, and generally behave according to the titles that either they assume for themselves or that others assign to them.

It's easier to get what you want when you know what it looks like or, at least, how it has to behave.

Titles, names and **nicknames** tend to embody expectations in simple terms. Names are often mandates for certain **levels of concern or respect**; carrying with them related powers or authority. Titles such as president, chief, professor, doctor, for example, simplify the meaning and understanding of human relationship. People holding such titles are expected to have credibility and are therefore easier to believe, listen to, follow, or obey. Names and nicknames are also suggestive of behavior types: Richard (formal), Dick (informal); Charlotte (formal), Lottie (informal); Biff (tough); Peachy and Jo-Jo (light-hearted), etc.

Names are fun to assume and play around with. They're the least expensive costume you'll ever find. Tricking yourself into going after what you want by assigning influential names to your problems and goals may be akin to child psychology, but it also might provide the positive view needed for success. It becomes easier to advocate for humanity if you personally assume the title of **humanist**, for example. If you dream of a vacation spent sailing to Belize, naming the project something like "Voyage to Paradise" and assuming the title role as captain would surely help you find lots of things to do to put the plan into action.

PERFORMANCE SPECIFICATION

Well-meaning, but apparently large or long-winded intentions are quickly changed into achievable plans when you break them down into small, bite-size actions and behaviors. The method here involves **turning the anxiety of wishing into the work of winning.** Once you have specified a detailed, bit-by-bit plan of achievement, all that remains for a successful conclusion is to follow the worksheet, perform the work, and enjoy what you're doing. The technique requires **getting more specific** about what the specifications for a winning performance include. In short, it's not too late to state in exact and measurable terms just what it will take to win.

Example: **Performance Specifications for a Long-Wearing, Low Cost Book Bag**: Lightweight (less than 3 lbs); Strongly woven, stain-resistant synthetic fiber fabrics; leather or plastic reinforced seams; unbreakable zippers; color-fast dyes; wide, non-slip shoulder straps; sits upright; easy-access compartments; capable of being accessed with one hand while being carried; variable use- carried as a handbag or worn as a shoulder bag; unobtrusive name tag; identifiable by detailing as a high quality product; interchangeable straps; non-rust metal connectors; color coordinated with palette of internationally projected fashion colors; retails for under $20.00 (manufactured for under $8.00); etc.

EIGHT POPULAR ACTION METHODS

What follows is a menu of commonly used methods and techniques for achieving or expressing concepts and ideas. Each technique has its own particular qualities, characteristics, and shortcomings in terms of its potential usefulness to your situations. Learning the basic information and developing at least the minimal skills for using many or all of these expressive communication and thinking methods provides a creative edge in problem-solving and goal-seeking.

A. *TRANSLATING AND DIGESTING*

Implementation often requires two critical creative abilities: transforming thoughts and intentions into various forms of language more appropriate to the situations at hand and reducing large or complex situations to smaller, easier-to-comprehend entities. Both skills are learnable; neither one is God-given. Learning to 'look at one thing and see another' takes practice, a sincere interest in the subject and its participants, plus a willingness to experiment.

B. *PUBLIC SPEAKING*

Speaking up, advocating a viewpoint, or attempting to exert influence on a group, all require public speaking skills. Acquiring a sufficient vocabulary and a reasonably correct knowledge of grammar to be able to clearly and credibly express your viewpoints in public are regularly required for many forms of implementation. Practice in writing and speaking won't make you perfect, but it will help in replacing imperfections with improvements.

C. GROUP DYNAMICS (Meeting Management)

Few implementation plans are totally exclusive of other players. Involvement with interpersonal or group dynamics is often necessary for getting what we want out of a situation. Meetings have therefore become an operational staple in most social relationships. Learning to accomodate the needs and concerns of others and developing the abilities to help a group think collectively, develop a common focus and behave as a team are not only basic to social organization, but are also generally useful creative behaviors.

D. WRITING

Learning to transcribe thoughts and concepts into some form of written language is invariably involved in achieving much of what we strive to attain in life. Legible expository writing, composed of a broad, correctly spelled vocabulary within a consistent grammar and sentence structure can credibly convey most message content. Like learning to speak in public, writing is also a primary mode of communication which improves with practice.

E. GRAPHICS

Sketches, photographs, charts, and diagrams are easy-to-understand ways to describe objects, relationships, or plans. Since "pictures" are closer to reality (more concrete) than the pure abstraction of words, writing and public speaking are normally augmented by some form of non-verbal visual or graphic aid. But, most people, falsely believing that drawings are kid stuff, discontinue drawing practice while 'growing up.' As adults, they soon realize the value of graphic skills, but tend to back off for fear of being identified as inept artists. Creative problem-solvers, seeing that it's not necessary to be "artistic" to improve their communication skills, continue to fearlessly learn the fundamentals of translating **visual thinking** into various graphic media.

F. MODEL-MAKING

Two-, three-, and now, even four-dimensional models are playing an ever greater role in visual communication. Models make it possible to preview reality before expending often great amounts of resources and energy to actually achieve it in its intended final form. Added to the model-making resource are the increasingly simpler-to-manage techniques of computerized model simulation and laser imagery. Learning how to quickly and efficiently produce model simulations of what you intend to achieve can become an asset to continuing success.

G. BODY LANGUAGE AND ROLE-PLAYING

One of the surest ways to get closer to what you want is to reach out and meet it half-way. "Become the thing!" "Play the part!" Let your actions speak for you. Show yourself and all others involved, that you are the best model of what you aspire to achieve or, at least, that you're trying your best to become it.

H. POINTS OF VIEW

Obviously, there are many, many 'other' ways than yours to look at life. Since there is a vast number of possible observation points about any focus, seeing only what appears before us represents but one of those myriad points of view. It's as if every viewpoint comes with its own set of filters that allow only certain things to pass and exclude all others.

Creative problem-solvers know that they can quickly illuminate new, or previously unseen, pathways to their planned destinations by changing their viewpoints (filters). Here are a few well-known examples:

H1. PRINCIPLES OF DESIGN

Design principles are man-made rules for composition, or putting things together; synthesis. Stemming from human observations and translations of Nature's operational "**common denominators.**"

The most commonly practiced design principles are:
Harmony: a <u>recognizable similarity</u> among parts of a group,
Contrast: a <u>recognizable difference</u> among parts of a group,
Balance: a <u>recognizable equilibrium</u> within a group,
Order: a <u>recognizable pattern</u> <u>of organization</u> within a group, and
Unity: a <u>recognizable oneness</u> or wholeness within a group.

110

Due to their derivation from the natural, physical world, these principles tend to produce satisfying and easily understood results when applied to any human synthesis or composition.

H2. *GESTALT PERCEPTION*

The psychology of human perception has been scientifically examined for decades. Gestalt studies (wholeness identity) produce still another version of design organization implications from the standpoint of how reality is perceived. The gestalt conclusion is that an object or group of parts is perceived as whole, only if the following requirements are met:

Similarity; something alike is perceived in all the parts,

Proximity; all parts are perceived as being close together,

Closed Forms; all parts are seen as being individually complete in themselves,

Good Contours; each part is enclosed or defined in an easily recalled configuration,

Common Movements; all parts obey similar organizational orders or patterns, and

Relevant Experience; viewers sense only what experience has programmed them to sense.

H3. *SENSORY SATISFACTION*

Problem resolutions and goals can more generally fulfilling when they offer a satisfying stimulus to all (or most) of the five human senses, not just one or two. The range of sensory satisfaction is broad. If getting what you want is often less than totally satisfying, it could be that only part of you is getting the attention you need.

Designing your achievements from the standpoint of delighting the senses can produce deeply satisfying results without necessarily being pursued or perceived in terms of hedonism or decadence.

H4. *HUMAN NEEDS*

All human wants, desires, urges, intentions, behaviors, and emotional expressions stem from a spectrum of satisfied and unfulfilled human needs. Satisfying and maintaining fulfillment of those needs, according to the pressure felt from them, is the source of human motivation. Any plan for solving a problem and/or reaching a goal can be more permanently implemented when it is made to respond directly to needs satisfaction.

H5. HOLISM

Akin to Gestalt theory, holism stresses the values of a **"both/and"** point of view, as opposed to the more commonly expressed **"either/or"** approach to dealing with life. A "both/and" viewpoint isn't so much all-inclusive as it is **open-ended**; permissive of serendipity and its happy accidents.

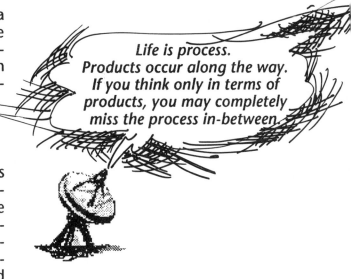

*Life is process.
Products occur along the way.
If you think only in terms of
products, you may completely
miss the process in-between.*

H6. LIMITATIONS

Thinking and operating in terms of limitations makes it possible to both stay within the bounds of acceptability, health, and safety as well as to stretch those bounds to their fullest. Limits define the realm of engineering: problem-solving and goal-seeking for efficiency, economy, practicality, improved reality. Creative engineers search beyond known limitations and design to extend them.

H7. RANDOM ORDER/CHANCE/CHANGE

The random order viewpoint is built on the fact that order, being an 'imperfect' human concept based on the observation of natural phenomena, is subject to variations and revisions. It follows the attitude that, since everything is subject to chance and change, design should be freed from all fixed laws, rules, and principles. And that in any case, out of the human need to perceive meaning from what is experienced, order will be seen to emerge from the products of chance just as it does as from those produced according to more traditional laws. Existential philosophy derives from a similar view.

H8. ART

Science seeks to discover; art expresses. When, in any synthesis, a discovered meaning or intent is expressed with influence and provocation, it is said to have 'art content.' Expressing the content of art is the product of both art and science. Creative problem-solving is both scientific and artful when it assumes the responsibility for providing provocative revelations in its various achievements and syntheses. Intolerance of what various people construe as provocative or mundane is a common problem accompanying this point of view.

112

H9. FAITH

The sentence which begins "I believe..." is the basis for the generic philosophy which keeps practically everyone moving in one direction or another. Whether your belief stems from national, social, religious, or personal values is less important here than its motivational ability to get you closer to where you want to be. Creativity begins with developing faith in one's self; in constantly developing an ever-greater sense of personal well-being.

Guidebooks for
Implemention

Critical Path Scheduling; Horowitz, Joseph; Ronald Press; New York; 1967

How To Make Meetings Work; Michael Doyle and David Strauss; Playboy Press; Chicago; 1976

Project Management with CPM, PERT, and precedence diagramming; Moder, Joseph J.; Van Nostrand; New York; 1983

Rapid Viz; Hanks, Kurt and Larry Belliston; William Kaufmann; Los Altos, CA; 1980

Stand Up, Speak Out, Talk Back!; Alberti, Robert E. and Michael L. Emmons; Pocket Books; New York; 1975

The Zen of Seeing; Franck, Frederick; Vintage/Random House; New York; 1973

Zen in the Art of Writing; Bradbury, Ray; Capra Press; Santa Barbara, CA; 1989

Evaluation

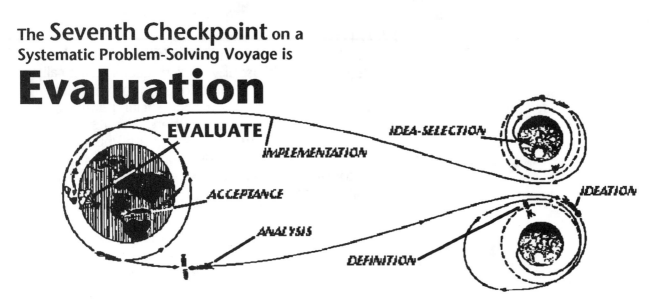

If you've come this far, you've already decided what you wanted and you went for it. Your problem may or may not be resolved; your goal may or may not have been reached. At any rate, it's over. And now it's time to make new plans. But, first, last, and ever ongoing, the question remains: "how well did you do?" You can now determine whether or not the ride was worth the cost.

Evaluation is the **pay-off**; a time for accounting; for comparing actions with consequences; for admiring achievements, detecting flaws, and making plans for improvement. Although it is like the first stage of Acceptance and somewhat outside of the main body of process, it's a mistake to think of the evaluative stage as a final or after-the-fact review. Actually, evaluation is many times more effective as an ongoing, concurrent checking device than as something to be considered only after "the damage has been done".

Evaluating accomplishment, whether in-process or afterward, is a time to look both backward and forward. Like life, evaluation is a continuous activity of determining the value of our joys and dreams, pains and heartaches. Whenever you consider it otherwise, you miss most of the show.

Language Guide
To EVALUATE PERFORMANCE
for a problem situation is...

...to measure accomplishment against expectations
...to see how much of your dream came true
...to determine the worth of your efforts
...to **benefit from experience!**

Methods for
Evaluation

Alternative Ways
for Determining Value and
Making Improvements
in Problem-Solving or Goal-Seeking

You don't have to wait until the end to judge how well you're doing right now. Stop occasionally to measure your progress along the way.

Evaluation methods and idea-selecting methods are somewhat alike in that they both have decision-making in common. Systematically speaking, any valid decision involves a measured comparison of objectives and deeds.

The basic concept of measuring value is to compare what you initially set out to accomplish with what you finally achieved and what you paid for the experience. Knowledge of that three-part relationship allows you to enjoy the true value of evaluation; the security of knowing how well you're doing at any moment and of being able to look ahead to continual improvement.

The **three essential requisites** of a complete evaluation are: **1. Measurable Goals, 2. Measured Achievements**, and **3. Proposed Improvements**. It's interesting to note that most academic grading systems include only the first two stages. In cases where course goals are fuzzy, only Step 2 (Measurement) occurs (in the form of an abstract, numeric or letter grade) leaving students "in the dark" regarding what went right or wrong or how to improve.

The most generally creative evaluation techniques are:

1. A PLAN FOR IMPROVEMENT
2. PERSONAL BEST
3. PAY (AND BE PAID) AS YOU GO
4. JURY OF PEERS
5. IN SUMMATION

A PLAN FOR IMPROVEMENT

Usually, after exerting effort toward achieving a goal, we become caught between a desire for a fair and accurate report of how well we did and the fearful anxiety of hearing how less-than-perfect we are. It's normal to seek praise and avoid hearing about what went wrong. Only the creative ones, intent on doing better next time, seek out both. Learning from experience is only effective when the cost of mistakes is emphasized, not ignored.

To effectively benefit from experience, the process of each major voyage should be well-documented and followed by a "de-briefing session" with the aim of knowing clearly what was achieved, not yet achieved, what went right, where we veered from our course, how certain methods worked and how others didn't fit at all, and what improvements are in order.

Since experiences are first felt (sensed) and then identified (known), measuring progress is normally slow. First impressions are invariably qualitative. This requires a translation- changing feelings, hopes or dreams and the fragmented souvenirs of travel from their normally qualitive form into quantitative, accountable terms. Because of our normal resistance to expending the required energy on something which seems so difficult or impossible, complete evaluations rarely occur. "I think I did O.K." or "I wasn't very happy with what I did" is the more normal replacement for a creative, derived plan for improvement.

Creative problem-solvers learn from their experiences. Others seem to re-learn the same lessons over and over.

BASIC EVALUATION GUIDE

A. GOALS

A **definitive statement of aims and intentions** is a necessity. All primary goals should be listed in the most **quantitative terms** possible, such as "I intend to average three in-depth interviews per afternoon," to write an average of one exciting chapter per month," to learn five new words every day," etc. When fuzzy qualities are included in goal statements, (terms like 'in-depth', 'exciting', and 'new' in the statements above), they need to be further translated into quantifiable terms. If you want to achieve them, you'll have to know precisely what you mean by each of them. The test question "how will I know when I get there?" still applies. For example, you can know just how 'exciting' your writing is by comparing it to a previously accepted exciting prose model, or by counting how many readers report having 'chills', etc.

B. ACHIEVEMENT
Accomplishments should also be measured quantitatively. If, in the end, qualitative 'feelings' are allowed to cloud and temper actual achievement or to rationalize failure, little improvement can be expected. Most commonly fuzzy, after-the-fact, emotions are hangovers from qualities that were never quantified into measurables in the first place.

Evaluation is a time for counting "all your blessings," in particular where new knowledge and skills were involved, and/or when attitudes and values were changed or introduced. Unforeseen contingencies should also be carefully noted in terms of the benefits they produced or the costs they added.

C. PLANS FOR IMPROVEMENT
After comparing expectations with attainments, it should be clear where improvements might be introduced next time around. Some measure of progress exists if merely one, relatively small, improvement occurs as a result of your evaluation plan.

PERSONAL BEST
Among the majority of athletes, competition has become a personal matter. Sports prowess is no longer a challenge between contenders to see who wins, but a challenge to one's self to see how much more each individual might accomplish.

In most sports, time and achievement records are established and athletes personally strive to meet and surpass those limits. It's called maintaining one's "personal best." Evaluating day-by-day performance is an important part of reaching one's personal best. It's also an excellent way to remain aware of your actual position relative to where you intend or expect to be.

The best way to record daily, step by step achievement is to use a journal, calendar, or progress chart. Such written or otherwise graphic documents become an excellent reference; useful for rapid review if it becomes necessary to explain your actions or when dealing with similar problems in the future.

If your implementation method was systematic, you've already been keeping regular tabs on your progress. For example, within a "time vs. task" chart, you could also include space for short evaluative comments which, afterwards, become reminders for improvements when planning future ventures.

PAY (AND BE PAID) AS YOU GO

Some people get anxious having to wait until 'lots of water has passed beneath the bridge' before stopping for an evaluative look at their progress. They prefer to keep up-to-date with where they are and how well they're doing by clearly spelling out which parts of their process are going well and which parts need improvement.

This approach, like others relying on using one of several variations of the time/task calendar, makes general good sense for those with motivational hang-ups. It allows them to glance at an always-up-to-date record and, with little effort, judge the feasibility of recommended changes in tempo or output. Plus, knowing where they are achievement-wise allows them to more consciously introduce behavioral changes where necessary.

Rather than waiting until you reach your destination for rewards or payoffs, why not get partial payments as you go? The incentive value of in-process improvements can make any trip more satisfying as well as keep you moving in your chosen direction. At the end of a designated period of time or acccomplishment, reward yourself according to how closely you have reached your intended target. When interim goals aren't met and rewards are few and far between, the "offending" behaviors will undoubtedly get scrutinized for improvement.

JURY OF PEERS

If, for some reason, you feel that evaluating your own performance is too personal and that you may not be able to judge yourself objectively, fairly, or accurately, you could aways ask someone else to do the 'dirty deed' for you.

The method involves making a deal with several trusted and respected colleagues to hear your case and hand down their value judgements.

Prepare for your 'day in court' by gathering together your project records and by inviting one or more people, whose opinions you respect, to serve as a panel of critics to hear your case. Be sure to **present your account in a systematic way**: Starting with an explanation of the initial project/problem situation, followed by an outline of the general content of your analysis and its resulting definitive problem statement(s); continuing with brief explanations of your best ideas; and how the best idea was selected and implemented; and ending with your final solution or achievement .

Have someone else make notes as your "jury" points out both the **strong points and imperfections** of your record. Don't forget to ask for recommended improvements where possible. Take **all** of their opinions and suggestions "under consideration," following those that seem crucial to personal improvement and saving the others for future consideration.

IN SUMMATION

Solving problems creatively and achieving what we want from life systematically are products of human intelligence and experience. They involve concepts and tools for improving human progress and the enjoyment of the life process. Systematics should help in the attainment of better results...greater success. It should never get in the way by being applied inappropriately.

In cases where detailed measurements and plans are clearly unnecessary, forget it. But, the least you can do is remind yourself that the essential purpose of a design process is self-management and the primary function of evaluation is **self-improvement**. Tailor your procedures and methods to your tasks. And, occasionally look backward to where you were, how you dealt with what you encountered, and how far you traveled. With what you discover, you'll be better able to judge how to move ahead with increased skill and confidence.

Guidebooks for
Evaluation

Evaluation Basics; A Practitioner's Manual; Kosecoff, Jacqueline B.; Sage Publications; Beverly Hills, CA; 1982

Goal Analysis; Mager, Robert F.; Fearon Publishers; Belmont, CA; 1972

The Nature of Human Values; Rokeach, Milton; Basic Books; New York; 1960

Theory of Valuation; Dewey, John; University of Chicago Press; Chicago; 1944 (1939)

Values Clarification: A Handbook; Simon, Sidney B.; Hart Press; New York; 1972

Ways of Growth; Otto, Herbert A.; Grossman; New York; 1968

PART THREE

Travel Enrichment

SIDE TRIPS

How to
Reap More Benefits
From Creative Problem-
Solving Journeys

**Sightseeing
Games
Travel Hints
Rules of Thumb
Tours and Travelogs**

Educational and Fun!

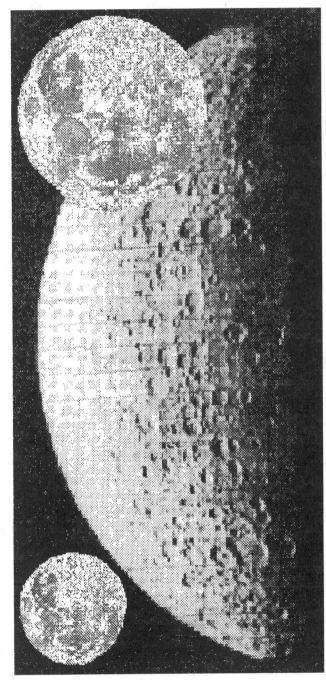

SIDE TRIPS can either misdirect your energies and take you off course or they can serve to enhance and enrich the value of your many journeys in life. It's all a matter of viewpoint... and skill in self-management. A creative problem-solver will evaluate all potential SIDE TRIPS to determine their possible value in relationship to current problem projects or goals. As when choosing from any menu of options or alternatives, process-awareness and decision-making skills provide the means to select only those extra-curricular options which seem to meet our **objectives** and to bypass others which seem anti-productive.

The life process is jam-packed with possibilities. **Living and enjoying a full, rich, and successful lifestyle by design** is the **ultimate human goal; the ideal existance.** To reach that goal while operating within our separate degrees of constraint, we each tend to envision a personal version of the meaning of true satisfaction and attempt to head in that direction. But, what works for us personally may be either equally desirable or downright troublesome to others. At times, our paths run peacefully parallel. On other occasions, our separate paths cross.

Some of the many options available within the life process get us closer to the realization of our ultimate dreams; some are mere diversions and set us back. If our overall dreams are fuzzy, it's hard to tell the difference between what might help and what could merely get in the way or lure us into forming new directions and plans. Either way, the result can be positive or negative and changing course is always related to the Navigator's 'best judgment.' Whether to **jump around** from one place to another or to **remain steady on a singular course** to a precise terminal is a matter of personal values and preference. Getting what we want from life requires careful steering and a regular review of our compass settings.

SIGHTSEEING:

Creative Tourism in the Life Process

Creative sightseeing can be educational and fun as well as productive. Practice with this creative form of open-minded, process-oriented activity is a proven method for learning new behaviors (thereby getting rid of or changing old, unwanted behaviors).

Allowing yourself to become a sightseer-tourist initially requires an adventurous spirit. Like any other form of new experience, creative sightseeing also requires conscious application and preparation. Although tourism is big business, tourists tend to be viewed negatively. We think of them as people who are "out of their home element"; as lacking the savvy and understanding of foreign customs and values; as being inept communicators, insensitive to their interim environment, inappropriately dressed, and in general, ill-equipped and unprepared...definitely not very creative.

Tourists are forever the butt of cartoons from the standpoint that their behaviors seem all wrong for the strange environments they enter. Yet, back home they were quite acceptable, behaving according to their familiar roles as clerks, managers, professionals, athletes, students, etc. Creative tourists must take on new roles (and behaviors) as linguists, diplomats, historians, geologists, social scientists, lovers of art and architecture, photographers, and gourmands. Unless accepted and planned for, those transformations are not likely to occur.

Although cautious restraint in new settings is normal, continuing to function with the same points of view and behaviors as before is like going to a theater wearing blinders and earplugs. Product-oriented persons will, of course, always remain concerned with getting there and returning to normal as quickly as possible. But, their superficial and soon forgotten travel treasures (snapshots, postcards, token "gifts", and "purchases") will never match the fresh, unique viewpoints brought back by process-aware sightseers.

Those who regularly enjoy the nuances of life's passing parade while at home will probably continue to discover and enjoy new wonders while on tour. Opening their senses to new experiences upgrades the value of their journeys by uncovering alternative relationships, deeper meanings, and new possibilities whereever they may visit. Again, it's just a matter of viewpoint.

How do you stop being a tourist and start becoming a 'creative traveler in life'? Answer: You become aware of and identify both types of behavior and start behaving more like the one judged as preferable. Here are a few guidelines for creative travel:

OPEN UP YOUR EYES AND EARS. TURN ON YOUR NOSE AND TASTE BUDS. FEEL THE AMBIANCE!! Awaken your senses to your environment. Become part of the scene and the action. Come into the reality of life from your position of observing it vicariously on the outside. Take part in the celebration. Jump off the curb and **join the parade** (at least occasionally)!!

DO TOUCH THINGS! How else can you know the true chill and glassy smoothness of Italian marble? Or the damp warmth and bristly coat of a camel's hump? Or the feel of a friend's hand in yours?

BECOME A TASTE TESTER! Of course, it's wise to use caution in making abrupt changes in diet. But, it's also enlightening to try new foods and flavors. Talk with the chef. Visit the kitchens, markets, and farms.

SCRATCH AND SNIFF! There's more to the olfactory kingdom than the smells of cologne, grilled meat, tobacco smoke and diesel exhaust. Search out the perfumes of life: the smell of rain; the incense of herbal seasoning; freshly laundered sheets; leather.

WHAT'S THAT SOUND? By consciously searching for the origins of both agreeable and unpleasant sounds, you'll open the door to appreciating many previously tuned-out sound-generating delights...and, above all,

ENJOY THE VIEW! Most of what we perceive in life is visual. Yet, we normally 'see' only a fraction of what our eyes take in. Learn to enjoy the myriad differences in color and light, the wide range of textural shades and shadows, the multitudinous patterns, shapes, and forms, the geometries and rhythms, around the edges and beyond the surfaces which define the real world. Stop looking and relearn how to see what is normally unseen or perceived only in superficial, abstract, and iconic terms. Make life an ongoing "world tour."

TRAVEL GAMES
The Play-Learning Method for Developing Creative Behavior

"Serious" game-playing goes beyond mere amusement; it has been clearly proven to be a valid, involving (hands-on) technique for learning all sorts of things, including creative behavior. Sadly, normal adults think of games as "kid stuff." They are too busy or too serious to play games. To creative people, life itself is a game. They play games all the time.

Children have always learned much about life and the 'growing up' process from the interaction they experience in the games they play. The need for practicing role-playing, problem-solving, and decision-making is inherent in almost all game designs. Game-playing, because of its appearance of freedom and lack of serious consequences, becomes an attractive, efficient way to reach beneficial learning goals and to quickly make a variety of evaluative improvements.

"Practice," of course, "makes perfect." But practice also means exercise; not just physical but also mental exercise. If you'd like to learn some new, creative behaviors or refine and develop older ones, games are an ideal medium to select for the task. Here's a sampling to try on for size. (Note: For other learning games and books on the subject, check the Learning Resources Centers of university libraries or specialty education and bookstores in your area.)

The "tricks" learned while playing specific games are generally useful in dealing with other of life's many challenges.

126

IMAGINATION

Allowing yourself the freedom to create mental images that go beyond the 'here and now' is an especially important creative ability. Developing that skill to the degree that it is always ready for use when needed takes practice. Try the following exercises to see how vividly your images can be. If the scenes you envision aren't truly convincing, try including additional sensory elements which might stimulate and appeal to more of your five senses.

A. Which animal does someone close by resemble? Picture that person, still fully clothed, but in that imagined animal form. Make your 'vision' more **real** by adding audible, tactile, and olfactory clues, too.

B. Imagine that you are very small, ant-size, and that you are walking around the surfaces of a fresh, fragrant rose. What do you encounter on your tour? What color is the rose? Describe the experience.

C. Imagine a swimming pool filled with chocolate custard. A three-foot wide cherry floats on top. How do you cope with such a crazy situation? Take a dip.

DIVERGE-CONVERGE

Widening out in all directions and **narrowing down** to a focal point are the two basic complementary thinking and behaving styles in systematic problem-solving. To be primarily one 'type' or the other is limiting, yet quite normal. A creative problem-solver is facile in both styles and learns the creative behavior of alternating back and forth between them as needed in the problem-solving process.

Imagine yourself standing in a barren, flat desert. The horizon is the same in all directions. Identify the details in the scene. Change the environment to that of the center of a busy urban downtown intersection with noisy traffic, tall buildings, and activity in all directions except downward. Pick a direction and take a short stroll. Notice as many details as you can, and return to where you began. Select another direction and take another stroll while noticing other kinds of things. When you return, do the same thing again in still another direction. Finally, look down into an open manhole. It's dark down there, but you do have a flashlight. Turn it on. What you see at the bottom relates to those things you saw while strolling down the streets. What's down there?

SEEING SOMEONE SLIP ON A BANANA PEEL IS BOTH SAD AND FUNNY!

Feeling pity for someone in a problematic situation and laughing at the humor involved in another person's misfortune represent contrary perceptions and values. Yet, given the proper attitudes and situations, both views are potentially constructive and creative.

Taking life seriously shouldn't imply a lack of humor or creativity and 'playing around' with serious subjects and situations shouldn't suggest immaturity. Seriousness is normal adult behavior; a natural outcome of growing up in a competitive society. It's easy to accept. Playfulness, on the other hand, isn't so normal or readily accepted as adult behavior. It's something that only a few 'rare' adults allow themselves to do in public. Still, developing the ability to see both the humorous and serious sides of life is prerequisite to creativity.

Humor is largely dependent on surprise; on quickly changing from the expected to the unexpected. Jokes and joke-telling capitalize on twisting normally serious situations into unexpected or abnormal conditions. Laughter is easily understood as the anxious, physically jolting, reaction to the surprise of meeting the unexpected. Creative persons can often be seen laughing to themselves as they mentally twist normal situations into strange new forms. They also find amusement in puns because a pun simultaneously links two meanings; one expected, the other unexpected.

Try these humor-generating games...just for fun!

A. Choosing clever 'punnish' business names, which sound like one thing, but mean something else, is a popular way to attract customer attention. Examples: WOK STARS (Chinese restaurant); CLIP JOINT (barber shop); ROUND UP (meat market); Etc. Now, it's your turn to find names for the following: a music store; a dental clinic; a men's clothing store; a computer salesroom; a regional airline; a car rental agency. Test the humor of your creations by noting the 'slow burn' reactions of several "victims."

B. Add new, humorously unexpected captions to several photographs in a magazine or newspaper.

C. Use tracing paper to playfully draw over a "serious" magazine or newspaper photograph of a famous person. Exaggerate their characteristic facial features, expressions and gestures as a cartoonist might do.

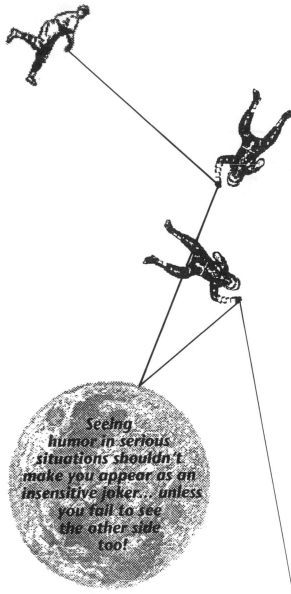

Seeing humor in serious situations shouldn't make you appear as an insensitive joker... unless you fail to see the other side too!

128

One person's solution is often another person's headache

PENNIES FROM HEAVEN

Disaster strikes everyone sooner or later; how often and to what degree is relative. We all tend to view life differently. Loss of a valued relative, friend, or possession can cause one person to suffer tragically, consumed with grief, for a lengthy period. Another might recover quickly and find the means to go on living freed from pain or anxiety. However, most of life's so-called "tragic events" aren't really so great a loss after the fact; things like losing a wallet or having a bicycle stolen, getting two parking tickets in a row, etc.

Making the most of every situation, whether beneficial or disastrous in appearance, is an essential creative ability. Instead of being "overcome" by tragedy, you can overcome **it** with some carefully designed mental game-playing. Instead of underplaying the loss; play up the opportunity for change and the possible improvements it offers. Practice on the following scenarios for a starter:

A. One morning you awaken to find that most of your clothing was stolen during the night. What now?

B. You've just been given a consolation prize of $500 instead of winning some special award you've been working so hard for. How might you turn your disappointment into an advantage?

YESTERDAY, TODAY, AND TOMORROW

A classic mind game for discovering who and what you are is played by imagining yourself playing the various parts in each of life's seven stages (as described in Shakespeare's "Seven Ages" monologue in *As You Like It*; Act 2): 1. Helpless infant; 2. School-child; 3. Lover; 4. Soldier; 5. Judge; 6. Senior; 7. Helpless Senile. Don your costumes, mount the stage, and play your roles, as only you can play them.

"And one man in his life plays many parts.
His acts being seven ages. At first **the infant**,
Mewling and puking in the nurse's arms.
And then **the whining school-boy**, with his satchel
And shining morning face, creeping like snail
unwillingly to school. And then **the lover**,
Sighing like furnace, with a woeful ballad
Made to his mistress' eyebrow. Then **a soldier**,
Full of strange oaths and beared like the pard,
Jealous in honour, sudden and quick in quarrel,
Seeking the bubble reputation
Even in the cannon's mouth. And then **the justice**,
In fair round belly with good capon lin'd,
With eyes severe and beard of formal cut,

And so he plays his part. The sixth age shifts
Into **the lean and slippered pantaloon**,
With spectacles on nose and pouch on side,
His youthful hose, well sav'd, a world too wide
For his shrunk shank; and his once manly voice
Turning again toward childish treble, pipes
And whistles in his sound. Last scene of all,
That ends this strange eventful history,
Is **second childishness** and mere oblivion,
Sans teeth, sans eyes, sans taste, sans everything."

HABIT BREAKER

Breaking a "bad" habit is much easier if you relax and
don't try so hard. The trick: **STOP STOPPING** and
**START STARTING. Find a good replacement habit,
which leaves no room in your life for the old one.**
You can test the logic of this method by brainstorming
a list of positive behavioral alternatives to the each of
following 'negative activities.' **Example:** My bad habit
of 'becoming angry when having to wait in line' can be
replaced by starting one or more of the following replacement habits: **A.** I won't wait; I'll telephone instead, **B.** I'll become friendly with other people in line,
C. I'll come back later when there is no line, **D.** I'll order by mail, **E.** I'll begin to enjoy being tolerant, **F.** I'll
ask someone else to wait in line for me, etc.

Now, it's your turn to play the game by generating at
least five alternatives to each of these "bad" habits:
1. Procrastination in fulfilling your obligations
2. Overeating fatty "junk" foods
3. Uncontrolled nail-biting
4. Never finishing what you start
5. Lateness for assignments and appointments

EGO STRENGTH AND FITNESS

Learning to strengthen one's own ego and to regularly
maintain its fitness is essential to creative mental
health. Everyone's ego needs an occasional hug. Instead of waiting for outside appreciation and/or becoming depressed if it doesn't happen, creative people
learn to pat themselves on the back. Here are a few exercises to build and maintain your sense of well-being.

A. Toot your own horn. Assemble the data for writing a
complete personal resume´. Try to include every important accomplishment thus far in your life.

B. Put on your best clothes and behavior (or just imagine it) and have some photographic portraits made.
Tell the photographer to 'bring out your best side.'

C. Imagine how greatly your family and friends would

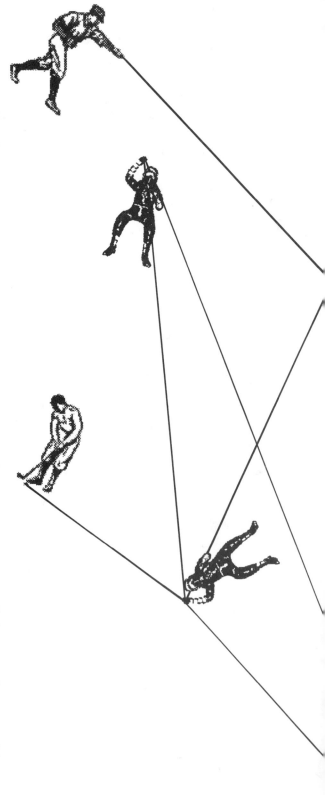

suffer when you are no longer there to contribute to their welfare. Write your own 'obituary' for local media. Include descriptions of your redeeming qualities and tell about your struggle to develop them.

PERSONAL HUMAN RIGHTS

Most people think of themselves as victims of many injustices in life and see themselves at the same time as 'too nice' to fight for what they know they deserve. Life is full of confrontations for fairness. The brave and the bold tend to be the winners; the timid and fearful are usually left 'holding the bag.'

Boldness and bravery aren't negative terms. They both engender respect. No sane, socially responsible person wants to behave aggressively or to hurt anyone. Whereas, giving up or giving in equals chickening-out; a definite negative. No one wants to sit by and be taken advantage of either. Being "nice" and getting what you deserve are not mutually **exclusive** terms. You **can** have both. The reason for giving up one for the other without a fight should be clear.

Training in **"assertive behavior"** is the key to getting what you want without hurting anyone's feelings. How do you say "No" when you really don't feel it's O.K. to say "Yes"? You assert your beliefs. It's like playing a game. Your chances of winning improve when you begin to know how to make **the right moves in tough situations**. It's also the same as for any other creative problem-solving situation. Until you define the problem (i.e., discover why saying "No" is better than "Yes" in a given situation), you're stuck with making up a lie, caving-in against your will, or being offensive or unclear about your needs. Going against what you feel is right will only turn to self-incrimination, aggravation, or hostility later on.

Let's see how you deal with these situations:

A. Quickly, and without manufacturing untruths, find three potentially 'good' reasons for saying "No" to a request from a fund-raising group to donate your support to an obviously important cause.

B. Practice making known your need to catch a soon-to-depart flight to an airline ticket clerk who is chatting idly on the telephone. What words will you use? Will you sound aggressive?...or assertive?

C. After you've just had your car serviced, vacuumed, washed and waxed for an important night on the

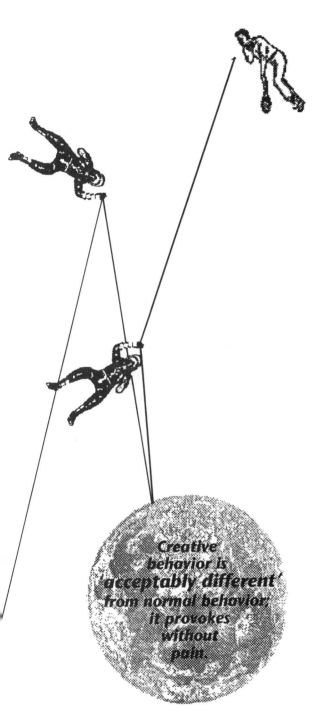

Creative behavior is 'acceptably different' from normal behavior; it provokes without pain.

131

town, a pal asks you for "a lift home." After saying "Sure", you discover that the pal also wants you to stop at the plant nursery to pick up four sacks of steer manure. How might you assert your rights without hard feelings and say "Sorry, Pal. I can't help you today"?

THE TWO OF YOU

It's fairly certain that thinking and feeling, our two primary human characteristics, relate to the left- and right-control centers in our brains. We know that healthy, holistic behavior depends on both of those aspects functioning as a well-balanced team- a systematic whole comprising an analytic and judgmental thought process partnered with an ability to enjoy experimental, multi-sensory data-gathering experiences.

Some human activities, like solving problems and making decisions, seem to be all thinking; i.e., primarily directed to flexing left-brain 'thinking' muscles. Other actions, like eating, walking, singing, and the like, appear to be totally sensory, or right-brain driven. Actually, to achieve a satisfactory, balanced, whole response in either case, both "sides" are required. The common concept that adults are left-brain thinkers is only partially correct. If we intend to achieve equilibrium in life and to respond creatively to any challenge, both our thinking "side" and our feeling "side" require continuous maintenance and interaction through practice. Think, act, think, act, think, act, think, act; that's the necessary rhythm; the **alternating current** of creative behavior. If you're not aware of it, you might get in trouble by thinking too long without acting or acting too long without thinking. Try keeping track of your personal **bi-modal rhythm** as you deal with the following situations.

A. In five to ten minutes, using any kind of music, write the lyrics for a short song about your town.

B. Announce what you've done and perform your song for a friend or two while beating out a percussion accompaniment with your hands.

PROBLEM-MAKERS

The standard, or typical approach to life is "if it works, don't mess with it" and/or "don't rock the boat." On the other hand, one of the unique attributes of creative problem-solvers is the fact that they're always on the lookout for ways to make things better.

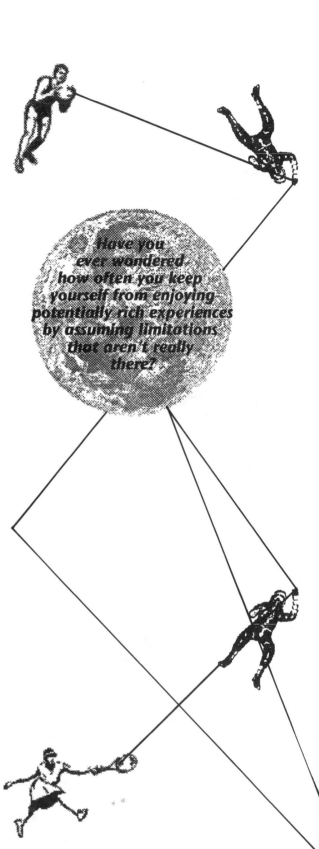

Have you ever wondered how often you keep yourself from enjoying potentially rich experiences by assuming limitations that aren't really there?

132

However, because of their curiosity (atypical behavior), **creative people** are forever 'rocking the boat' in search of problems to solve. Their "constructive discontent" provides the impetus to dub them as **problem-finders** first and **problem-solvers** next. Impatient with the status quo, they are always "messing around" with what "don't need fixin'" in search of some part of it that 'could be better.' How good are you at being a problem-finder?

Find three ways to improve the following items which already seem to be "working just fine". Make drawings to depict your best idea for each case.
A. A screwdriver; B. A banana; C. Parking lots; D. Movies; E. Today.

YOU CAN'T DO THAT IN PUBLIC

The fear of being criticized for breaking some unknown law or for being less than perfect accounts for much of our conservative reluctance to behaving more experimentally. We all have our own ideas about the limitations regarding what we can and can't do. Many of those 'restrictions' we establish for ourselves are often unnecessary; brought on by some imaginary fear or as a subconscious reaction to a forgotten negative past experience.

Some of the things we allow ourselves to do in the secure privacy of being all alone, we'd never condone in public. Singing in the shower is a classic example. Why is it enjoyable to play at being an opera star at home but, when others might hear us, a cause for timidity and shame?

Where does the inner 'authority' to behave so 'outrageously' as to sing in public without a trained voice come from? The answer: from your own control center. We provide our own authority to either stand back or to fearlessly perform (practice.)Test your ability to overcome imaginary barriers with these games.

A. Unplug your answering machine and/or don't pick up the phone for 48 hours. Take note of what worries you about doing this "irresponsible act."

B. Turn on some music and ask someone to dance with you. If no one's available, dance alone. What seems to be holding you back?

'Ignorance of the law is no excuse' for holding yourself back from discovering what the true limits of the law might be.

C. Watch for news anouncements and attend tryouts to play a minor role in a play production of a local theatre company. Which imaginary personal bugaboos will have to be destroyed to pull this one off?

BETCHA' CAN'T! - BET I CAN!

When we read a book, attend a lecture, or listen to "words of wisdom," it's amazing to discover how much of what is being presented we already know. But, if asked beforehand, we'd probably 'own up' to very little. It's just easier to deny our limited knowledge than it is to prove its extent. We tend to mislead ourselves into believing that since we aren't experts, what we do know can't be worth very much. Such poor logic has a negative carry-over when we need to call on our personal data storage banks for various bits of information during problem-solving.

Although the challenges in the following games may sound initially unrealistic, working to provide responses can help you gain confidence in your existing 'vast' general knowledge of many and various subjects.

A. Betcha' can't "identify 50 flowers by name!" (Note: You'd probably recognize the names of 150 or more if you saw them listed.) What's stopping you? Was a time limit stated? Were proper botanical names asked for?

B. Betcha' can't "name all 50 States" in the U.S.A.! (C'mon. Are there really any states you haven't heard of yet?) How about their capitol cities?

C. Betcha' can't "find 20 good reasons" for buying life insurance! (Who's going to be the one to define what a "good" reason really is?)

LEARNING BY DESIGN

One way to learn about anything is to try teaching it to someone else. Teaching is a "forced-method" of learning because it immediately requires filling in lots of gaps in your own understanding before going on to explain what you know to others.

For example, you can personally learn to develop a particular new behavior by designing a game to help someone else learn that behavior. First, select a simple behavior that you'd like to develop yourself. Then find the means for getting others to practice it in a gaming context. You'll soon learn what that behavior is all about and how to practice it yourself.

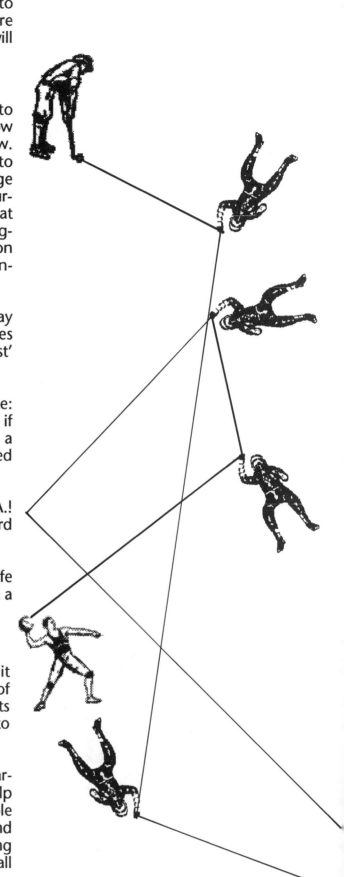

Searching for one kind of thing leads to the uncovering of other kinds of things.

A. Design a playground game for 12-year-olds where, via their involvement, they begin to develop social responsibility.

B. Devise an indoor physical game which uses musical videos to teach teenagers the values of teamwork.

C. Outline the contents and primary rules for an adult boardgame which emphasizes the importance of using process and method in situations requiring design and invention.

D. Adapt a popular boardgame like MONOPOLY, which teaches real estate acquisition, money management, bouncing back from hard luck, orderly process, and a host of other behaviors, to become a training aid instead for learning about urban problems such as pollution, crime, noise, overcrowding, waste management, etc.

Guidebooks
for Game Design and Game-Playing

Creative Growth Games; Raudsepp, Eugene w/ George P. Hough, Jr.; Jove (Harcourt, Brace, Jovanovitch); New York; 1977

Design Games; Sanoff, Henry; William Kaufmann Inc.; Los Altos, CA; 1979

Serious Games; Abt, Clark C.; Viking Press; New York; 1970

The Five-Day Course in Thinking; deBono, Edward; Pelican; London and New York; 1968

The Metaphorical Way; Gordon, William J.J.; Porpoise Books; Cambridge, MA; 1971

POST CARDS

Thoughts and Sage Advice extracted from Travelers' Logbooks

Creativity is an intentional activity...something available to everyone...not a birthright for a select few.

Thinking of ideas and inventions is easy. The hard part comes when you try giving them form and putting them to work.

Save all your solutions. The unused answer to one problem can often be used in other similar problems.

There are no 'dumb' questions or 'wrong' answers.

If you haven't been there before, take it easy until you get to know more about the place.

After selecting the best from many options, there may still be a better way.

Chance or guesswork can sometimes produce better results than systematic procedure. But, you can't depend on them.

Liberal imagination is a good partner for conventional wisdom.

If it works, it may still need fixing. If it doesn't work, it may need to be thrown out.

When one path is blocked, try another. Usually, there are many ways to get to the same place.

Trust yourself. 'Gut reactions' grow from experience.

Hard work and use of system are no guarantees of success. They merely improve the odds for achievement.

When there is only one option, there is no choice.

Unpleasant memories and bad habits are best removed by new experiences and new behaviors.

A first idea may be the best idea...or the worst idea, but hopefully isn't the only idea.

Making something look easy to do can take a lifetime of practice.

It's important to keep the entire picture in sight while examining any one of its parts.

Complete and well-kept process records are often the most valuable end-products.

Instead of waiting for the pot to boil, turn up the heat. Products accumulate faster when the focus is on process.

Right and wrong, Good and Bad are relative terms. Their meanings change from moment to moment and from situation to situation.

Change is the only thing that never changes.

Reality is a matter of opinion. Each of us sees things differently and what appears to be can be misleading. We must all learn to navigate alone and in the fog.

One person's solution is another person's headache.

Problems are rarely solved completely, but tend to be re-solved over and over again.

Inner peace is being able to laugh at one's own mistakes. Education is learning to not make the same mistake twice. Intelligence is avoiding mistakes in the first place.

Jumping to a conclusion can save time, but it could cost a fortune. At least take a look before you leap!

Preconceptions and assumptions account for most of the minor decisions made in our lives by efficiently eliminating several problem-solving stages. They also account for much of life's grief.

Creative vision is the ability to look at one thing and see many things.

Learning and inventing call for opposite points of view. Learning requires relating what we don't know to what we already know. Inventing requires turning what we already know into something yet unknown.

Since all things are interrelated, everything is both related to and different from everything else. To discover something unique about anything, try asking how it's like something else.

The surfaces of things are like mirrors which feed back reflections of ourselves. To gain insight, we must break through those surface mirrors.

We're always doing our best. If we could do better, we would. Stepping outside of ourselves for evaluation is the key to improvement.

Taking a break is sometimes the best way to get something done.

Most of the limits and barriers that hold us back are imaginary and of our own making.

Truly original thinking is a lonely business where no one else thinks as you're thinking. A person with a brand-new idea is automatically a minority of one.

Scientists can be every bit as 'original' as artists, just as artists can be procedural and methodical.

Creative behavior is 'acceptably different' from normal behavior; it provokes, but does it painlessly.

Balanced behavior requires opposites acting with a 'both/and' kind of teamwork: rigid flexibility and wide-eyed focus.

Systematically following a single path to a selected goal doesn't rule out dancing all along the way.

Two heads are only better than one if you can get them to behave as one.

TRAVEL TOURS and TRAVELOGS

Companion Guides for Creative Behavior

The joy of having helpful travel companions and the best of equipment can make any trip memorably pleasant. Here are some general travel helpmates in the form of guidelines, rules of thumb, and attitudes to consider packing along with the rest of your gear on upcoming problem-solving tours.

GOALS AND OBJECTIVES: A Necessary Duo

Goals are general destinations. **Objectives** are the components of goals. In general, goals aren't directly attainable. Instead, we attain goals by satisfying the objectives which collectively define them. Even if you plan to get rich quick by directly playing the lottery, you've still got to meet some objectives: finding the money to buy the ticket, going to the vendor, selecting the number, etc. Example: If your goal is to become an architect, you don't just become one by striving for the end result. You must focus on satisfying all the requirements (objectives) such as courses of study, degrees, internships, licencing laws, etc. associated with professional practice.

If a goal's objectives aren't clear or if you have no way of knowing when they've been reached, the whole business gets very confusing. The secret to clearing things up is in making objectives measurable. 'Losing five pounds a week' is a measurable objective for reaching a weight loss goal of twenty pounds within a month. The goal statement 'I want to lose **some** weight' isn't measurable. It's a start, but the indefinite term 'some' defies evaluation.

The hardest objectives to measure (quantify) are qualities; things like 'I want to get <u>smarter</u>' or 'I want to generate <u>lots</u> of <u>good</u> ideas.' Indefinite words like 'smart', 'lots', and 'good' must first be defined before they can be reached. If 'good' is defined as 'quick and economical,' "good ideas" become much easier to recognize and achieve. "Lots" could mean just about any amount until quantified as a specific limit, such as "more than ten." Words like "smarter" are trickier, but still definable and quantifiable. Becoming smarter could mean "having all the pertinent facts" or "solving problems more efficiently" or "wasting half as many resources" or all of the above. Once known, it's suddenly easier to work toward "getting smarter."

SELF-HYPNOTISM

We give ourselves the authority to behave in certain ways. We allow ourselves to do certain things and not others. We abide by many sets of rules and laws in life, but first of all, we obey our own rules. We are "the masters of our fate." Creative behavior is a function of self-control; an intentional, voluntary activity.

Mastering one's fate involves **will power**; an expression relating to how forcefully we maintain obedience to our own concepts of right and wrong. If we think of ourselves as being 'weak-willed', we tend to mean we don't often get what we intend; that we've established certain rules to live by but still allow ourselves the freedom to break those rules without penalty.

Having a handle on self-control is essential to behaving creatively. It involves **joining the conscious level with the subconscious**. This requires reaching deeply inside our inner consciousness in order to make behavioral observations and leave behavioral messages.

Behavior-directing messages to our inner selves are best implanted during a state of intense relaxation; a deep-sleep condition associated with deep breathing. Many books and audiotape aids are available to help you learn how to arrive at the necessary hypnotic state and benefit from it. Ask your reference librarian for assistance. **Self-control** has many names, including focus, meditation, sleep-learning, prayer, Zen, Hatha Yoga, trance, Mind Control, Scientology, EST, etc., but it always boils down to being some variation of **self-hypnotism**. Its potential power is awesome.

TOLERABLE CRITICISM

Sincere concern for the feelings of others and a healthy ego strength make both the giving and taking of advice more agreeable. But critical comment, no matter how well-intended, usually hurts the recipient, at least a little bit. Painless criticism is a rarity. Another important creative behavior can be developed by learning both how to give criticism as well as how to take it. Neither one comes naturally or easily; both take practice.

The trick to giving criticism as painlessly as possible is to **sandwich your critical comments within outer layers of positive reinforcement** and to follow up by **tagging on a ray of encouragement**. Example: "You're doing much better now. <u>Pay a bit more attention to your spelling</u>. It'll make your good ideas easier to read. If you'd like more help, please ask."

When advice comes from someone else and is offered to you, make sure to consider it "with a grain of salt" i.e., **accept only what appears to be positive** and reject the rest instead of carrying it around as an unnecessary load. If you receive no encouragement or ray of hope from your critics, **add a few boosts and pats on the back** of your own.

THE JOYS OF CREATIVE PROBLEM-SOLVING

Sometimes outside pressures force us into negative situations. The best advice is to make the most of them. At other times we agree to do things which go sour and we have to pay the piper until our debt is paid. The positive approach is to wait it out while making plans for change. When the way is clear and you still find yourself unhappy at your work, make some changes as soon as possible. If what you're doing makes you sick, stop doing it altogether. If procedural, methodological problem-solving, and goal-seeking are just too stringent to swallow, relax and enjoy a more casual alternative. Life is too short to experience it in misery.

If you want to feel better about what you're doing and perhaps get a few highs and chuckles along the way, all you need to do is join in the fun that's already in process. It's easy...just use your imagination to put on your party glasses.

142

Change or remodel your working space into a more desirable living-working place...

Your surroundings have a strong influence on how you think and behave. If they're not conducive to making life more enjoyable, they need changing. A workplace should help you want to be there; not encourage you to leave. You don't need to get carried away with expensive, time-consuming renovations in order to change the feeling of a workplace into something more suggestive of its importance to you. Sufficient work surfaces and comfortable seating are basics.

Dress the part, collect the props, play the role...

If you're wearing the wrong costumes, using all the wrong props, and/or behaving in ways contrary to the role you aspire to play, it's time to make some changes. Once again, read your "script", follow the"stage directions" you've written and design some ways to become more like the character you wish to portray.

Invite other interesting and encouraging pals to attend your ongoing party...

Why burden yourself with the negative thinking of those around you when you can change all of that? (If thy friends and associates offend thee, cut them off!) Instead you can begin to benefit from other, perhaps new, friends with more upbeat, constructive viewpoints. It can be exciting to seek out role models who clearly enjoy life and to try following their examples.

and don't forget to replace any no-longer useful habits with fresh, positive behaviors...

Use calendars and schedules (maps) to guide you through difficult passages; remain conscious of your intentions and destinations; stay positive about your intentions; keep the stages of problem-solving process in mind so that you don't have to rely on others to get started or to stay on course; be daringly guarded, yet cautiously bold and...*a creative problem-solver*.

Index